Winning Habits

A unique and groundbreaking analysis of how to succeed in equestrian sport, this book unpacks the winning habits of successful equestrians to form a toolkit for readers to develop their own winning habits.

Applying psychological understanding in peak performance, this book is bolstered by interviews with top contemporary professional show jumping athletes to explore and show how leading equestrians have interpreted various methods and built them into approaches for their own training. Theoretical concepts such as mindset, deliberate practice, focus and flow are broken down and translated into practical steps for a more powerful and effective way of thinking, training and performing. Renowned equestrian mental coach Annette Paterakis reveals factors of success, as well as answers common questions, from building lasting confidence to responding to failure. Smashing the myths of talent and hard work, Paterakis offers a refreshing take on mindset, focus and approach to success both in and out of the show ring.

An essential read for anyone who would like to learn about or improve their mental game, this book is uniquely suited for equestrian riders, coaches and other athletes, as well as offering supplementary reading for applied sport psychology courses.

Annette Paterakis is an equestrian mental coach and author who has worked with athletes all over the world, from amateur to Olympic level. She specializes in helping equestrians create a mindset that builds confident, consistent and powerful performances in sport and life.

Winning Habits

How Elite Equestrians Master the Mental Game

Annette Paterakis

Routledge
Taylor & Francis Group

LONDON AND NEW YORK

Cover image: Shannon Brinkman photo

First published 2022
by Routledge
4 Park Square, Milton Park, Abingdon, Oxon OX14 4RN

and by Routledge
605 Third Avenue, New York, NY 10158

Routledge is an imprint of the Taylor & Francis Group, an informa business

British Library Cataloguing-in-Publication Data
A catalog record for this book is available from the British Library

Library of Congress Cataloguing-in-Publication Data
Names: Paterakis, Annette, 1985 – author.
Title: Winning habits: how elite equestrians master the mental game / Annette Paterakis.
Description: Milton Park, Abingdon, Oxon; New York, NY: Routledge, 2022. | Includes bibliographical references and index. | Identifiers: LCCN 2021037640 (print) | LCCN 2021037641 (ebook) | ISBN 9781032068398 (hardback) | ISBN 9781032068381 (paperback) | ISBN 9781003204084 (ebook)
Subjects: LCSH: Horse sports. | Horse sports--Psychological aspects. | Horsemanship and training equestrians.
Classification: LCC SF294.2.P38 2022 (print) | LCC SF294.2 (ebook) | DDC 798.201/9--dc23
LC record available at https://lccn.loc.gov/2021037640
LC ebook record available at https://lccn.loc.gov/2021037641

ISBN: 978-1-032-06839-8 (hbk)
ISBN: 978-1-032-06838-1 (pbk)
ISBN: 978-1-003-20408-4 (ebk)

DOI: 10.4324/9781003204084

Typeset in Bembo
by MPS Limited, Dehradun

Contents

Introduction

Introduction

My journey to becoming the mental coach I am today started in 1993, in the Netherlands, when I had my first riding lesson. I was hooked straight away. I loved the smell of horses (believe it or not), being around them and taking care of such beautiful animals was now the only thing on my mind. Soon after I got my first pony and I started competing at small shows. I was often clear in the first round, which got me to the second round, the jump-off against the clock. I was totally present and connected with my pony, we were a team and having lots of fun together. As a result, we were racing through the arena, like our life depended on it, taking such tight turns I would hit my shoulder against the jumps. The thrill, the adrenaline, the excitement – I loved it! I was very competitive and within a few years, I began riding more ponies and started conquering the regional, national and, eventually, international shows.

During the first few years of competing, I was placed almost every weekend. The jump-offs were my strong suit. If I was clear in the first round, I would give it my absolute all without a shred of fear in the jump-off. As a result, I was confident and I quickly moved up the levels to compete internationally. Soon after, however, I paid the price of skipping some valuable steps and landed with my feet firmly back on the ground. I couldn't understand what had happened. Only a few months ago I was winning and now I couldn't seem to finish even the first round anymore. My ponies were stopping, refusing to jump the jumps and after two refusals I would need to leave the arena. Getting to the finish line became my new goal and I often failed at that. I was devastated and confused. Slowly but surely my confidence started crumbling down until I was crushed with self-doubt and frustration.

I didn't know what to do. My trainers told me to keep at it, telling me, "You will get there eventually." So I did, but I struggled. My results became very inconsistent and with that, my joy for riding disappeared. I had not noticed how my previous success had made me hungry for more and better results. It was like an addiction. I was addicted to success, but I wasn't getting it anymore. The more

DOI: 10.4324/9781003204084-101

I focused on getting certain results to give me that shot of dopamine, the less I focused on my connection with my horses. I loved them, don't get me wrong, but I was so focused on proving that I was a good enough rider, that I forgot what it was all about. I had forgotten why I started riding in the first place.

Determined and dedicated as I was, I kept at it. I was not going to give up. After high school, I worked for various show jumping stables in the Netherlands and Belgium. I worked as a rider, training and often competing their horses as well as managing the yard, mucking out stables, and looking after the horses. The fact that these were not my own horses and they needed to get sold added even more pressure for me to do well at shows. My results remained inconsistent, doing well one day, failing miserably the next. At one point, after another disappointing show, I decided that I would either figure out a way to stay cool under pressure and ride like I knew I could ride, or I would quit altogether.

As double Olympian McLain Ward told me in our interview together, "You have to be at your lowest point, struggling so much. That's when you open up to new ways and you will do anything [to succeed]." I was now at that point, and I started to realize that unless I deliberately took action, nothing was going to change. A belief that has since become my life mantra and it rings as true in show jumping as it does in life in general. Luckily, I found a great mental coach who helped me understand the basic principles of the brain under pressure and how to create more control over my mind when at the shows. Things started to make sense and I increasingly learned to exercise control over my own body and mind. However, I still had a long way to go. My confidence was still dependent on circumstances and results. Good show – a bit more confidence. Bad show – no more confidence. I knew I wasn't there yet. I still had questions and I still felt I had to learn more to get to where I wanted to be.

During this time, I decided to continue studying from home, so I could balance riding and running my own yard with getting my degree. While I thoroughly enjoyed my Applied Psychology studies, it was tough to combine it with riding, mucking out, grooming, driving to shows, and taking care of seven to eight horses all on my own. In other words, these were *very* long days.

As Steve Jobs so famously stated, "we only connect the dots looking backwards." Now looking back to 2012, although I didn't know it at the time, my journey had led me to this very moment. I realized I had to change something. I was unhappy, frustrated, and tired. I didn't feel in control of my own life or my future, so I made a difficult decision. I stopped riding full-time. I stopped so I could start something new, something that would enable me to use all this experience in a positive way. As I finished my studies and got my Bachelors's degree in Applied Psychology, I realized how much I enjoyed coaching and training, so after many months of contemplation, I decided to take a big leap and start working as a mental coach.

I continued my mission to find more answers – and better answers – to the question "How can riders not only excel under pressure, but also stay happy along the way?" I enrolled in different training courses and devoured books. I became obsessed with peak performance, success, and living an extraordinary life. This innate desire to learn was reflected in my reading. Books like; *Talent Is Overrated, Mindset, Black Box Thinking, Grit,* and *Peak* had a profound impact on my beliefs about talent and what it takes to become successful.

I started applying all kinds of tools, exercises, and new ways of thinking to my own life and when they worked and proved effective, I translated them to the equestrian sport. Confident in my methods, philosophy, and approach, I started passing on all this experience, knowledge, and passion to my clients. I wrote my first book *Keep Calm & Enjoy The Ride* and my clients not only got the results they were after, but most importantly, they told me how much they enjoyed riding again.

Learning more about concepts like talent, growth mindset and deliberate practice, challenged my beliefs about success and how to get there. I had held onto certain beliefs for a long time and they hadn't served me at all. Beliefs like "you need talent to succeed," were now overruled by research into peak performance and what the determining factors to success really are. After reading the stories of many successful athletes, finding common themes, and spotting patterns, I was intrigued. Could these theories hold up in equestrian sport?

Even though I had many ideas about what I believed to be the most important factors in achieving high-level success in show jumping, I had never reached that level myself, so I couldn't know with absolute certainty. I decided to find out. Through interviewing the riders at the top of the show jumping sport, I wanted to learn what their journeys had been like. I wanted answers to questions such as: What are the determining factors or characteristics that make the difference for these riders? What do these riders have in common? If other riders apply the same habits, patterns and ways of thinking, can they move forward and become successful as well?

I was very excited by the idea of doing this research and sharing my findings in my second book. Truth be told, the idea of interviewing my idols, people I had been looking up to all my life, was thrilling but also daunting. I walked around with the idea for a while until, at the beginning of 2017, I met up with Noelle Floyd at the Winter Equestrian Festival (WEF) in Wellington, Florida. I had been writing biweekly blogs for her online platform for a few months and now she wanted to talk about new ideas for our work together. One of her ideas was to interview top equestrians and write articles for her magazine about them. Determined and quick to the chase, Noelle helped me to overcome my procrastination and organized for me to interview Laura Kraut within three days! I took it as a sign and huge honor, as Laura is one of the highest-ranked female riders in the world.

I had three days to come up with the right questions, study interviewing techniques and make sure my recording app worked on my phone. I woke up the morning of the interview feeling really nervous. I applied the techniques I had been sharing with my clients to myself and by the time I was driving through Wellington, I felt excited and ready. Laura was kind, down-to-earth, easy-going, and open to share all of her thoughts. It remains one of the most in-depth and fun interviews I have done so far. Just like that, I lost my stage fright and I couldn't wait to interview more riders. My journey had begun, and little did I know what a thrill and a joy it would be.

The research into peak performance has been a personal journey for me and interviewing these top athletes has taught me about so much more than just riding. I have learned how their experiences, habits, and mindsets have shaped their lives and their success. I discovered that you and I have the potential to thrive in the same way if we apply the same ways of thinking to our everyday lives.

The Athletes Interviewed for this Book

All the athletes I interviewed are professional show jumping riders. The information below is up to date until the time of publication.

Laura Kraut:	As mentioned above, Laura is one of the leading female riders in the world and has an impressive resume with over 100 Grand Prix wins, an Olympic gold and silver medal and a World Championships gold and silver representing the USA.
Lorenzo de Luca:	Lorenzo is a Grand Prix rider and regular on the Italian team, won Grand Prix's and has competed at World Equestrian Games.
Janika Sprunger:	The ever-charming Janika Sprunger was so kind to make time for me during the Knokke Hippique Horse Show. (We ended up chatting for 2 hours, which felt like a wonderful talk with a dear friend.) Janika competed at the Olympic Games in Rio ending up 6th with team Switzerland and 37th individually.
Daniel Deusser:	Not long after, I was coaching a client at Stephex stables and managed to interview Daniel Deusser. Daniel is a regular on the German team and works for Stephex Stables in Belgium. Some highlights of his career are, finishing 2nd during the FEI World Cup Final in 2007, in 2014 winning both the German championship as well as FEI World Cup Final, in 2015 winning a silver medal at the European Championships with the German team

as well as a Bronze medal at the Olympics in Rio. Daniel has ranked world number 1 in 2017 and again in 2021 and has won the prestigious Grand Prix of CSIO Aachen in 2021.

Laura Klaphake: A rising star for Germany, Laura Klaphake has already an impressive track record for her age. Some highlights are team gold medal at the European Championships in 2010 (with the ponies) and 2014 (Young Riders) and a bronze medal with the team during the World Equestrian Games in Tryon in 2018. As well as other very impressive wins and results.

Jonna Ekberg: Young Swedish star Jonna Ekberg is a former rider for the Stephex team. She competes up to 5-star level and has represented Sweden during Nation's cup teams as well as ridden in the biggest show jumping arena's in the world like CSIO Aachen and Falsterbo.

Piergiorgio Bucci: Piergiorgio (also known as PG) is an Italian Grand Prix and Nations Cup rider. An important team member for Italy for years, PG has won a team Silver medal during the European championships in 2009 as well as various Nations cup's and Grand Prix titles. Although I have worked with both Jonna and PG regularly over the past few years, through interviewing them I learned new and valuable things about them, their journey, and their approach with horses.

Edwina Tops-Alexander: Edwina is an Australian Grand Prix rider, Olympian, and one of the top-ranked female riders in the world. Juggling a thriving riding and business career together with being a mom, Edwina was understandably too busy for a face-to-face interview but kindly replied to my questions and sent her answers over email. Some highlights of Edwina's career are representing Australia during three Olympics in Hong Kong (2008), London (2012), and Rio de Janeiro (2016) – with two top ten placings. She was the first Australian to qualify for the Final of the World Equestrian Games in 2006 and won the semi-final. In addition, Edwina is two times overall winner of the Longines Global Champions Tour and winner of the LGCT Super cup in Prague in 2018.

Cian O'Connor: Irish Olympian Cian O'Connor divides his time between Ireland, mainland Europe, and the USA. Individual Olympic Bronze medalist and two-time European medalist, Cian has won many important titles and has been a consistent member of team Ireland on over 116 Nations cups in his career so far.

McLain Ward:	With an impressive track record, McLain has won two Olympic Gold and two Olympic Silver medals and countless other championship titles such as individual Pan American champion in 2015 and FEI World Cup Final champion in 2017. From April till June that same year, McLain managed to become Longines FEI World ranked number 1.
Olivier Philippaerts:	Member of the famous Philippaerts family in Belgium, Olivier is the youngest rider to ever win the legendary Spruce Meadows Grand Prix in Canada. Olivier is considered a consistent 5-star rider and team member for Belgium. Coincidentally, Olivier happens to be based very close to where I used to live for 11 years in the east of Belgium.
Jeroen Dubbeldam:	It's safe to say Jeroen is the most decorated show jumping rider I interviewed (and perhaps ever) with an individual Olympic Gold medal, he is also individual and team World Equestrian Games champion, European champion, and multiple times Dutch champion. Though Jeroen is considered a real championship rider, he too has many other titles to his name including the winner of the prestigious CSIO Aachen Grand Prix in Germany.
Maikel van der Vleuten:	Maikel and I started off at the same shows during our pony years and I still remember him, already at that age, winning most classes on most weekends. Maikel continued his career with many individual successes as well as contributing to many nations' cup titles, including a bronze medal at the Tokyo Olympics in 2021, an Olympic Silver medal and World Equestrian Games gold medal with the Dutch team.
Markus Fuchs:	Lastly, Markus Fuchs is a former Olympic rider for Switzerland, now a trainer. I didn't ask Markus the same questions I asked the other riders, rather I talked to him with a more specific topic and question in mind, which you will discover in Chapter 1.

I'm deeply grateful for each rider's generosity with their time and their openness to share their successes, as well as their struggles. These riders are all incredibly busy and competing every single weekend, I can't thank them all enough for making time to talk to me!

Throughout this book, the riders I interviewed and I, regularly refer to different levels of competition within the international Show jumping sport. For those of you not familiar with the equestrian sport, here follows a brief explanation of the show jumping levels of competition.

On the national level, the types of competition vary between countries, but at the international level competitions are run by the international equestrian federation, or the FEI (Fédération Équestre Internationale). Within the international types of competition, each level is ranked with a star or multiple stars. One star being the lowest level and five stars being the highest. A course at five-star Grand Prix level exists of 10–16 obstacles of about 1.60 meters high and up to two meters wide.

My Work as a Mental Coach

Since I started as a mental coach in 2012, I've worked with athletes all over the globe, from amateur to Olympic level. As my heart is still very much in the Equestrian sport, it brings me great joy to be working with riders and empower them to be the best version of themselves, in and out of the saddle. I not only help them improve their performance, but also aim for them to enjoy the journey as every road to success, comes with its inevitable roadblocks and difficulties. I encourage my clients and all the riders I encounter, whether during workshops abroad or through my online training program, to apply many of the learnings in this book. From stepping into a growth mindset, to training in more deliberate ways to becoming more confident and consistent.

Since I finished my Bachelor's degree in Applied Psychology, I have continued to educate myself through various training courses to continue finding better answers. My approach to improving myself so I can help my clients improve is an intuitive one, whenever I find myself not having good enough answers or ways of improving my client's questions; I go out to learn why. This is perhaps the biggest difference between me – a (mental) coach, and a sport psychologist who will take a more scientific route to answer questions.

My approach has always been very practical, hence the Applied Psychology studies. My theory is that knowledge is great but unless we apply it and adjust our daily habits and routines, not much is going to change. This is why the findings in this book are called Winning Habits, not Winning Traits. Even our mindset is an accumulation of thousands of thoughts and beliefs that we have repeated in our heads over and over again. In essence, our mindset, the way we train, our focus, getting into a flow state, dealing with failure and even our confidence are all essentially habitual ways of thinking we have acquired over time.

Therefore, before diving into the chapters, learning how to change our habits is key to successfully applying the findings in this book.

Creating New Habits

When I was 17, I started working with a mental coach myself and he explained to me how the brain works under pressure and why I made silly or at times, very big mistakes when at the show, as opposed to at home. This really helped me realize that my mistakes had little to do with my riding abilities and much more to do with how my mind worked. He then went on to teach me a simple breathing technique that I had to practice every day. At first, being someone who is always busy and on the go, this sitting down and "doing nothing" was challenging for me. In fact, it took me many years to make it a daily practice. However, after a few days or sometimes weeks, I would return to this simple exercise, as I knew how much I benefited from it. And I still do today. Even though I'm not competing anymore, I use it because I need to stay focused on all the work I do and I want to be as productive as I can be. Apart from that, it has a very beneficial impact on my immune system. What I've learned over time is that, like with any good advice, lesson or wisdom, it's not enough to just get the concept. We need to integrate it into our day-to-day lives so we can keep reaping the benefits. As a result, over time I have focused more and more on creating daily habits. Those clients who have also successfully incorporated these habits into their daily lives are the ones who always report progress in many different ways. They report feeling much more content and happy about their journey, feeling more motivated, more in control of their riding, more consistent, confident and above all, more focused and connected with their horses.

In the next chapters, we will unpack the winning habits the riders I interviewed and many successful athletes, musicians, entrepreneurs, and people in business (just to name a few) have adopted. There might be habits you have already integrated into your daily routines, but perhaps there will be other habits you'd like to change. Changing our habits can be challenging, where do we start? Let's explore together how we can successfully change or adopt a new habit.

Step 1.
The first step is to **decide what exactly it is you want to change**. If your thoughts and language are vague, you will most likely get vague results. For example, we often think to ourselves "I should do this" or "I really should stop doing that," but this kind of language is not clear enough to make change happen. Instead, decide what you want to achieve and what that looks like once it's become part of your daily routine. Let's use an example to bring these steps to life. Imagine you have decided you want to spend less time on your phone and more time reading a book. Your goal could become, I will not use social media during the first 30 minutes after waking up and I will spend 30 minutes reading a book before going to sleep. Once this new goal has become a

habit you expect to sleep better at night and be more focused, rested, and productive during the day.

Step 2.

Step two is to determine **why you want to change something** or not.

Having a clear why can help you stay on track. Using the example above, the reasons why you want to change this habit and follow-through are; you want to change being on social media and spend this time reading because you want to learn something interesting instead of wasting time scrolling through other people's lives. Also, you have learned that being on your phone before bed can interfere with your sleep and you'd like to get back to the deep sleep you used to have. Lastly, you are getting distracted easily while competing lately, and (as you'll learn in this book) reading helps to increase focus.

Step 3.

Once you have decided what you want to change and why, you now want to **become very aware of your current habit**. Become aware of the moments you spend the most time on your phone. Take a few days or even a week to just observe and/or note your current behavior patterns. Perhaps you spend most of your time on social media first thing in the morning, when feeling bored or overwhelmed, and before going to sleep. Whatever (unhelpful) pattern you have established, just observe it instead of judging it. Feeling bad about your behavior will not help in the process of changing it.

Step 4.

Now, the most important step is to **prepare like a pro** and set yourself up for success. First of all, decide when you want to start your new habit, at what time in the day you will execute these habits, and what could potentially distract or keep you from following through. You have decided you want to start tomorrow by not being on your phone in the morning and reading before going to sleep. You know your self-discipline when waking up and still being half asleep is not optimal so you decide to charge your phone in another room. You also decide on which book you want to read. As you take the book of the growing "books to read one day" stack and place it next to your bed, you feel excited about your new goal. Lastly, you add a little post-it note on your bedside table with "Good morning, remember to leave your phone charging and stay present during this first half an hour."

Step 5.

The next step is to **set tiny sub-goals**. When changing our habits, we often feel like everything needs to change at once. We need to exercise every single day or eat only healthy foods. But this approach doesn't work for most of us. Instead, build on small steps of improvement until you have reached your target. In this case, you could decide to start with leaving your phone for 5 minutes in the morning and start reading one page every evening. After one or 2 weeks you can increase this time and the number of pages. Until you get to leave your phone for 30 minutes and read for 30 minutes in the evening.

Step 6.
Before we begin, one final but important thought. When creating new habits, **commit to progress not perfection**. It's better to stick to the habit and do it for 2 minutes, than not doing it at all. If you repeat your new habit at the same time every day, like brushing your teeth, eventually it will become a habit. In case you do fall off the wagon and forget for a few days, no problem, just get back on track. Every day and every moment offer a new chance to create change.

How to Read this Book

This book is for anyone who would like to learn, improve, and up their mental game. Whether it's in the equestrian disciplines, in another sport, or in any area you would like to improve upon. You may be a show jumping rider at the beginning of your career or a CEO wanting to increase your confidence to grow your business even further. Whatever your background, there are no rules as to how to read this book. You may prefer to dive right into a chapter you want to learn more about, like confidence for example, or maybe you prefer reading it front to back in one go (kudos to you). I do encourage you to read the whole book, as every chapter relates to another and so only then will you be able to see the full picture.

Some of you are avid readers, and some of you may not be that fond of reading, but you just want to learn more about these riders and find out if there is a chance you too can improve yourself and perhaps even become as good as your idol. In case you feel a little intimidated starting this book, know that just by picking it up, you are already training your brain and mental game. In fact, reading is a very effective tool to increase your focus, crucial to deliberate training and success, as you will find out in Chapter 3.

Even if you don't use the tools I share in each chapter (though I hope you will), I know this book will help change your mindset and help you realize how much potential you actually already possess. Every victory was first created in the mind. Every mind has the potential to envision the biggest dreams. Let's dive into the minds of the greats and in the process, build our own.

In this book, I'm going to show you how a life of winning habits and becoming the best version of yourself, is very much in reach.

1   Mindset

I believe that it was the mindset I had adopted on my journey as an equestrian that greatly determined the trajectory of my career and life. As you will read in this chapter, the limiting mindset I started out with caused me to feel frustrated and demotivated as a young aspiring athlete. As a mental coach today, I see the same happening for many of the athletes and people I work with. No matter the background, age or level, their underlying mindset has negatively influenced their confidence, performance, excitement and enjoyment. This group has one glaring commonality; a fixed mindset. Through her research, Carol Dweck, a leading psychologist and researcher into achievement and success, realized there are two fundamental mindsets that can greatly influence our determination and resilience on our path to becoming the best we can be: a fixed mindset and a growth mindset.

In the context of this book, *Mindset* is the belief you have created about your own potential, what you believe to be possible, and based on that, what motivates and drives you. In a nutshell, when in a growth mindset, we believe that our potential is limitless and the possibilities of succeeding are numerous, this creates a drive and motivation to continuously improve and grow. In a fixed mindset one believes that our potential is bounded and determined by talent; the possibilities, therefore, are restricted and uncertain and the motivation to succeed comes down to seeking validation and proof that one is good enough. Most often, we are neither in one mindset or the other, but we have acquired a combination of both fixed and growth beliefs. For the purpose of explaining the impact of these mindsets, however, I will portray them separately and explore what it looks like when we have adopted one or the other. Just keep in mind that even an expert like Carol Dweck mentioned, "in truth we're all a mixture of the two."

In her bestselling book *Mindset*, Dweck asks the following question, "If you had to choose, what would your preference be; loads of success and validation or lots of challenges?" The answer to this question is quite telling about the extent to which you have adopted a fixed or a growth mindset. To be clear, neither is right or wrong but the mindset you adopt has a huge impact on how you perceive success, failure and feedback. How can it be that a simple, often subconscious, difference in mindset can have such an important impact on one's career, relationships, choices,

DOI: 10.4324/9781003204084-1

behavior, performance and trajectory of life? Let's explore the difference between the two opposing ways of thinking, a fixed versus a growth mindset.

Fixed Mindset

The two mindsets are like two different worlds. Enter the fixed world and you believe that you either have what it takes to succeed, or you don't. You believe that your core abilities are fixed and perhaps you can improve them with training to some extent, in essence, you are either a natural or you are not. You either have the necessary talent to succeed or you don't. This creates a rigid and inflexible way of thinking and you feel the need to prove yourself. You constantly feel the need to be validated. You need proof that you have what it takes to become a successful rider. As a result, the outcome, your performance and the end results are your main concern. Coming out of the arena with a mistake is very upsetting as it may be proof you are not good enough. Therefore, you are scared of failure and making mistakes, which often leads to the desire to be and ride perfectly, make your performance look effortless and be able to sustain this perfection at every level and in every class you enter. Only then you will be happy and able to enjoy the ride. In order to keep proving yourself this way, you stay in your comfort zone. You prefer to stay safe so you can maintain this level of excellence or at least avoid making mistakes. You tend to identify yourself by your results and you take mistakes, failure and feedback very personally. When you win, you are successful and when you lose, you are a failure. Needless to say, this is not sustainable; you will make mistakes and when you do, you tend to dwell on them instead of learning from them and thinking about how you are going to fix them. Ironically, your performance plateaus as a result or even drops over time and you keep making the same mistakes. You don't feel in control over your own destiny, instead, you either feel blessed, special and confident when things go well and doomed, unlucky and worthless when they don't.

To a show jumping rider or any athlete for that matter, the fixed mindset creates great pressure to succeed and to prove good enough. This often translates into worrying, over-thinking and with that, becoming distracted when in the arena. You're focused on the results (which reside in the future), not on the process, which means your mind jumps forward into the future instead of staying in the present moment. As a result, you are more "in your head" than you are feeling the horse beneath you and so-less connected with your horse.

Let me elaborate. Imagine you go into the arena. You jump fence number one, two and three when on your way to jump number four, you hear the pole drop on the ground behind you. Straight away you feel this disappointment as you think, "I can't believe I had that one down, what a stupid mistake!" Now you are one stride before jump number four and you realize you are too close, you pull and sit back, but it's too late, this one comes down too. Now you are really upset because you just eliminated your chances of you qualifying for the next round. You go from being in the past, upset about the mistake you made, to the future, not being qualified, instead of being in the present moment feeling what is going on underneath you.

In essence, a fixed mindset stimulates a focus on results, perfection and the need to prove yourself. It increases fear of failure, overthinking and worry of making mistakes, which creates negative self-talk and distraction. Conversely, enjoyment, motivation and confidence all rise and drop with the coming and going of validation.

To some of you, this may sound a bit dramatic, but in all honesty, this is exactly how I felt when I was a professional rider and I know many clients who feel or have felt this way when in a fixed mindset. If you recognize yourself in elements (or all) of the description above, you too may have subscribed to (parts of) a fixed mindset. This doesn't mean you have a weak mental game or that there is something wrong with your thinking, it just means you have adopted some unhelpful beliefs along the way. As we will see at the end of this chapter, judging yourself when you recognize some fixed traits showing up is not doing yourself any justice. Instead, let's go on a journey and learn about the opposite position of the growth mindset.

Growth Mindset

Stepping into a growth world means you are much more focused on improvement and becoming the best version of yourself. Sure, the results matter, but they don't define you. The way you ride in the ring and your results are feedback of how well you have trained, they are a result of your preparation and processes. Therefore, instead of being solely focused on results, you are much more interested in, if not intrigued by the process. You believe that you can change, grow and progress through training and experience. Though you may start with your own unique talents and characteristics, your true potential is unknown. With the right kind of training and many hours of that practice, anything is possible. It doesn't mean you are guaranteed to be the next Jeroen Dubbeldam, Beezie Madden or McLain Ward, but unlike believing your abilities are set in stone, you believe your full potential is unknown. Based on this open mindset, not knowing your full potential means you constantly push yourself to become better.

The key quality of the growth mindset is its passion for learning, the desire to keep stretching yourself and to constantly push outside your comfort zone. Failure is not something to avoid, but rather something to learn from. In fact, in a fixed mindset, when failing, your first response is that you are not good enough. Conversely, in a growth mindset, failure means your *training* is not good enough. Often failure is not even viewed as such, but rather that you are challenging yourself and therefore improving. In this way, some might even welcome failure.[1] As constant improvement is the main aim, result-based goals are not there to prove something but merely to challenge yourself to become better. The mere joy of riding, improving yourself and your horses are the main motivator and source of enjoyment and fulfillment. As a result, your confidence and motivation to train are stable and sustainable.

In a nutshell, the difference between the two worlds is that in a fixed mindset you aim to prove yourself, whereas, in a growth mindset, you aim to improve yourself.

Let's get inspired and look at two examples of a growth mindset Dweck provides in her book *Mindset*.

"Boxing experts measure protégés fists, reach, chest expansion and weight in order to identify the "naturals." Muhammad Ali failed these measurements. He was not a natural. He had great speed but he did not have the physique of a great fighter, he didn't have the strength and he didn't have the classical moves. In fact, he boxed all wrong. He didn't block punches with his arms and elbows. He punched in rallies like an amateur and he kept his jaw exposed. He pulled back his torso to evade the impact of oncoming punches, which Jose Torres said was "like someone in the middle of a train track trying to avoid being hit by an oncoming train, not by moving to one or either side of the track, but by running backwards. Sonny Liston, Ali's opponent, was a natural. He had it all, the size, the strength and the experience. His power was legendary. It was unimaginable that Ali could beat Sonny Liston. The matchup was so ridiculous, that the arena was only half full for the fight. But besides his speed, Ali's brilliance was his mind. Not only did he study Liston's fighting style, but he closely observed what kind of person Liston was outside of the ring: "I read everything I could where he had been interviewed. I talked to people who had been around him or had talked with him. I would lay in bed and put all the things together and try to get a picture of how his mind worked." And then he turned all that against him. Ali's victory over Liston is boxing history."

If Ali had had a fixed mindset, he would have felt defeated before even starting the fight. He would have worried about his performance and all his shortcomings. He would have doubted his unique approach and technique. Instead, being in a growth mindset he did not focus on what could go wrong, he focused on what he could control and how to get it right. Like a butterfly, its beauty lies in the preparation, the time spent in its cocoon, fighting to get out prepares the butterfly to spread its wings and fly. Similarly, Ali focused on the process instead of the results and prepared himself in every way possible, relentlessly training his body and mind, going over every detail to out master the "talented" favorite.

Dweck continues, "Michael Jordan wasn't a natural either. He was the hardest working athlete, perhaps in the history of sport. It is well known that Michael Jordan was cut from the high school varsity team, we laugh at the coach who cut him. He wasn't recruited by the college he wanted to play for (North Carolina State). Well, weren't they fooling? He wasn't drafted by the first two NBA teams that could have chosen him, what a blooper! Because now we know he was the greatest basketball player ever, and we think it should have been obvious from the start. When Jordan was cut by the varsity team, he was devastated. His mother told him to discipline himself. Michael understood and left the house at six in the morning to go practice before school. At the university of North Carolina, he constantly worked on his weaknesses – his defensive game and his ball handling and shooting. The coach was taken aback by willingness to work harder than anyone else. Once, after the team lost the last game of the season, Jordan went and practiced his shots for hours. He was preparing for the next year. Even at the height of his success and fame, after he had made himself into an athletic genius, his purposeful practice remained legendary. For Jordan, success stems from the mind. "The mental toughness and the heart are a lot stronger than some of the physical advantages you might have. I've always said that and I have always believed that." Other people don't always believe that however. They only see the end product, the physical perfection that led to his greatness."

Would Michael Jordan have become the icon and idol he is today if he had had a fixed mindset? Imagine what would have happened after those setbacks, being turned down over and over again. Focused on his failure would he have gotten up early the next day to deliberately and purposefully train his skills? It's easy to see the end product and think, "oh but he is a natural," "he worked hard yes, but surely he was also more talented than the rest." Can you say with 100% certainty that those athletes you consider "talented," were actually gifted from day 1? It's not about what mother nature has given us, it's what we do with it that makes all the difference.

In show jumping, there are similar examples of riders who didn't start off with that natural ability. These riders worked very hard to compensate for their lack and found a way to turn their weaknesses into strengths and against all odds, become successful.

Take Markus Fuchs for example. The Swiss showjumper has been to five Olympic Games and he was part of the Swiss team to win the silver medal at the 2000 Olympics. When growing up, however, Markus was not considered to be the most talented rider. In fact, his brother Thomas was the one with all the "talent" and "good feeling." Markus told me "I was never as gifted as him. For 25 years, I was convinced I was not good enough as a rider. On top of that, staying cool under pressure was never my advantage. But I just continued and eventually I got an amazing horse, Tinka's Boy." In order to compensate for his lack of talent and ability to stay cool under pressure, Markus did everything he could to improve himself. He got different kinds of trainers, worked on his physical training and trained his mind with a technique called Autogenic training. I have to admit, I had never heard of this kind of mental training so I looked it up. In summary, Autogenic training is a desensitization – relaxation technique developed by the German psychiatrist Johannes Heinrich Schultz.[2] It uses a combination of self-hypnosis techniques, helping the body to relax. By repeating the same phrases with a focus on relaxing the body and heartbeat, it helps to self-regulate the central nervous system, letting go of the fight or flight response to become more relaxed and focused. Determined to find a solution, a better way, Markus tried new things to improve himself.

That said, Markus still felt that at important moments when the pressure was on, he couldn't make it happen and as he called it "failed." But there were also moments where he did manage to curb the nerves and thrive. Markus explained "I was in Gothenburg for the World Cup final and I believe I was in the lead after the first round. I still remember I went to the stables to lie on a straw bale to practice my mental training. I was so relaxed after that, that I nearly missed the second course walk. But it worked, my horse [and I] won."

Although an incredibly hard worker and perhaps too hard on himself, in hindsight Markus admits that he was not as consistent with his mental training as he could have been. He explains, "Because there comes a stage where you win a lot, you really think you are good but then when the pressure was there I still became too nervous again." We need to take into account the element of time when all this took place, however. Mental training was not at all part of a riders training (it still barely is today), in fact, it may have even been controversial at the time. But Markus was open-minded enough, dedicated to finding solutions enough to try something new and with great success.

Perhaps his success ironically caused him to ease his mental training, something I see happen all the time with my clients. If Markus would have been more consistent with his mental training, he may have continued his success and ended his career on a more positive note. However, hindsight is a great thing and it doesn't take away from the fact that during all those years Markus experienced self-doubt, he did not give up, he continued to persevere, work hard and find ways to get better and that is, without a doubt why he became as successful as he did.

Markus' example summarizes the core of this chapter in that it's not talent, but training that makes or breaks a performance and career. Whether that deliberate training applies to riding skills, mental skills or any other skills, doesn't matter, it's the continuous and consistent small steps we put in every day that makes the difference over time. If Markus would have merely focused on the results, he may have stopped riding much earlier than he did. Instead, he focused on the process and pursued solutions to strengthen his weaknesses. The importance of continuous, consistent training to create consistent results cannot be stressed enough. Of course, it would have been easier if Markus had the ability to thrive under pressure by nature (if that is a genetically influenced trait), but his track record proves the point that it's possible to reach big goals and success when staying patient, open-minded and applying the right kind of training.

Equestrian Talent

Before we continue I'd like to first dive deeper into the underlying, limiting belief of the fixed mindset. Because it's this myth that **without talent one**

can't succeed, that is the root cause of the problem. It is this belief that causes equestrians, athletes, children, parents, lawyers, musicians and people in business to name a few, to feel not good enough, unworthy and defeated. It's this belief that has caused many incredible people to give up and to never share their greatness with the world.

I too had subscribed to this myth for many years. After embarking on my research into peak performance, however, I learned (by reading books like *Talent Is Overrated*, *Bounce*, *Mindset* and *Peak*) that talent is by no means a determining factor to success. In fact, researchers like the late Anders Ericsson take it a step further and conclude they have not found any proof so far that talent actually exists. Nevertheless, I was very curious to find out how the top riders I was about to talk to viewed talent in relation to success.

Trying not to be biased by my own views, I asked most of the riders I interviewed about his or her beliefs around the importance of talent versus training. Based on that, I wondered if they believed that they had always been talented and had always had the abilities they have today or if the skills they have, were learned.

Starting with Laura Kraut, I asked her about her views on talent. Did she believe a rider needs talent or is training more important? Laura answered, "I believe it is person specific. If you are a rider with not the most talent but a serious work ethic and a very, very, good calculating brain, somebody who can be focused and a quick thinker, I think you can teach them to become as successful as they are willing to be. I think sometimes they can outdo the talented ones."

Edwina Tops-Alexander interestingly took it a step further when asked; *what in your view is the defining factor in this sport, talent or training?* "I think training and being able to understand why the mistakes have happened and to be able to work forward to get better results. Of course talent makes all the difference but without the discipline it won't get you to the top."

Laura Klaphake is more of the opinion that out of talent and training, there is no stronger "preferred" element – it is a balance of the two. "I think both are important, it's everything together. If you have talent but no training it's not good. If you are training a lot and you have no talent it's also not good. It's very important to train hard to become a good rider, but I think you can become very good with talent and good training."

McLain Ward offers a clear and concise response when asked about his view on talent. "I think talent is one of the parts of the recipe. But I see a lot of talented riders that don't put it together."

In his usual no-nonsense style, Cian O'Connor offers his view on what he believes is most important. "You need a certain amount of talent, you can't make a monkey an Olympic champion! But hard work can get you very far, like my late grandfather (Dr. Karl Mullen) used to say, "success is reward for effort." For example, if you have a talented guy who is lazy or who goes to the bar or who is just less interested, he won't survive. If you have a less talented guy who wants to work hard and gets up early and is prepared to put in the hard slog, he will get much further. This gets proven time and time again. Read any book about sports, look at all sports across the world. If you take two boys both 20 years of age, one is a national genius but he's lazy and likes to go to parties and the other one is less good but works hard, I think the less good guy will get there."

Olivier Philippaerts has an impressive track record of success, especially for his young age. I asked him whether he believes his success is due to talent or training. "To put a percentage on it, I would say 80% was due to training and 20% to talent. With the right system and the right training you can go a long way. For sure you do need some talent in this sport, but I know people that, with the right training, came a long way and with the right people you can get there as well."

Jeroen Dubbeldam shared an interesting view on talent. "Of course you need talent. Without talent at all you don't get there, but for me, in my case I would say its 60% horsemanship and 40% talent." Jeroen points out here the importance of not just any training, but the skill of "horsemanship."

As we will see throughout this book Jeroen often refers back to this ability, which in his view is the most important skill for an equestrian rider. The dictionary defines horsemanship as "the skill at riding horses," but amongst equestrians, this term reaches much further than that. It's about understanding the horse, understanding how they think, what makes them tick. Understanding their nature and always keeping in mind that the horse is a wild animal that doesn't owe us humans anything. The fact that they are willing to work with us, is something a rider should always appreciate and never take for granted. Therefore, becoming a team with your four-legged partner is a process that should be based on respect and trust. In a way, horsemanship, like leadership is just another skill that can be learned and trained over time.

Finally, I asked Maikel van der Vleuten what he believes is more important, talent or training. In line with the other riders, Maikel replied, "I believe that to win at the highest level, you need both, it's as simple as that. But a rider with a lot of talent that thinks too easy about it and doesn't work hard for it will fail. A rider with a little less talent but who really works for it and manages to put it all together can make it." I couldn't resist and had to ask what percentage he would allocate to each. According to Maikel, that would be 70% talent and 30% training.

Let's summarize these answers. Six out of the eight riders whom I asked the question about talent versus training answered that they believed in a combination of both talent and training. Almost all of them replied with the example of a hard-working but less talented rider still being able to make it to the top. Two of the riders, when pushed to choose between talent and training, replied that they thought training is more important, but still acknowledged that talent plays an important role. Three riders answered by allocating a percentage to each. The importance of possessing talent was 20% from Olivier, 40% from Jeroen and Maikel answered 70%. No one rider allocated 100% to talent, which again indicates that even when you are blessed with some kind of genetic advantage, it is by no means a guarantee to success.

So far, we have learned that talent is considered helpful, but without the right training, team and process in place, it will not guarantee success. However, I still felt like diving deeper into the topic of talent with these riders. From the eight riders I asked about their views on talent, I asked six of them whether they believed they had always possessed this talent. Surprisingly four out of six answered that they did not.

If you see McLain Ward riding in the arena today, you see effortless, smooth, brilliant horsemanship at work. Imagine my surprise when he talked about his lack of talent growing up. "I was terrible in the beginning you know. I rode ponies awful and didn't look like I had much talent so it was a rough start. When I was 12, 13 things got better and better and then it started to go in a good direction." It goes to show it's deceivingly easy to watch an "end product" of relentless training, a symbol of effortless success and call it talent. But without seeing the full picture, you can never know whether a performance was delivered based on talent or training.

Similarly, Cian O'Connor explains how training is almost like a discovery or better yet, sculpting process for talent. "I wasn't the most talented when I started off. There were guys ten times better than me. But somewhere there's talent in there and training brings it out."

Surely Olympic champion Jeroen Dubbeldam has always possessed this talent I thought, but he replied, "A lot of people would say I did, but I don't think so, not like a lot of other riders did. I won the Olympics when I was 27, 26. It's the biggest thing that you can win in sports. But I feel now I am a better rider than I was then, strange enough."

It's always fascinating when an Olympian admits they are better today than they were when they actually achieved peak success, but clearly Jeroen was not merely driven by results and fame and continued to hone his skills. A clear piece of evidence he has adopted a growth mindset and not just when it comes to his own development and abilities as a rider. Jeroen has been successful with so many different horses and I asked him about his secret to this consistent success. Jeroen's reply is quote-worthy; "Because you don't get a top horse, you make a top horse! You start with a horse that maybe has possibilities and maybe one horse has more possibilities than the other one. My biggest results in my career I have achieved on horses that everyone was yelling at and nobody liked. You make a horse. Of course, some horses are easier to make than others and some horses have more natural talent than other horses, but you can train a lot and make a top horse."

Laura Klaphake considers herself lucky, as she was able to achieve similar or better results but with less time spent in the saddle than other children her age. She contributes this advantage to talent. She said, "I think I am lucky, when I was younger I was talented. Other kids were riding lots of horses a day, but I wasn't riding everyday because I had school, I had my other sport, I had my friends, so I was busy and wasn't riding as much as others."

But then Laura continues: "For sure when I was a kid, I was not always having the perfect distance. I always tried but sometimes it was not working out but then I had the ambition to train. This isn't working, so now I have to train more or I have to ride more shows to get more experience. It was also training I think, it's a mix of the talent, the training and ambition."

It seems like all these riders had a certain talent, hidden somewhere, but only with training, did this talent fully come out. This triggers the question, what is talent for an equestrian rider? And where does talent come from? If talent were a natural ability, it would suggest it is something we are born with and can trace back to our genes.

Angela Duckworth is an infamous psychologist whose research sought to answer the question, what is the secret to outstanding achievement? In her book *Grit* she explains the following: "There is no single gene for talent, grit or indeed any other psychological trait! ... On the contrary, dozens of research studies have shown that almost all human traits are polygenic, meaning that traits are influenced by more than one gene." "In total, the human genome contains as many as twenty-five thousand different genes, and they tend to interact with one another and with environmental influences in complicated, still poorly understood, ways."

This evidence alone would suggest that there is no such thing as an "equestrian" gene; rather, that there are separate genes that interact together and are influenced by the environment (such as the right horse, training, circumstances, etc). This raises the next question, what are these separate components or traits that we define as "talent" and that are crucial for the show jumping rider? I asked these riders; *how would you define talent for a rider?* For quick reference, I've highlighted the key components of the answers.

Laura Klaphake says, "I think the most important thing is to have **feeling for the horse**, in the ring and also in the warm up. You really have to feel how the mood is of the horse and then when you have this under control, I think it is important that you **have a very good eye to see a good distance**."

"It's a difficult question." Olivier Philippaerts admits, "The feeling of riding is something you have from nature, **you need to be able to feel the horse**."

Jeroen Dubbeldam agrees, "**It's a feeling, a feeling** for the rhythm, **eye for the fence**, that's a talent, to go to a fence with a horse that's maybe difficult to ride, but you feel what to do to make it happen. The feeling for the rhythm in the course, the rhythm going to a fence, the feeling taking off the ground and landing, that is something natural."

I couldn't help but dig even further and ask, *you say it's something "natural" but seeing a distance to a fence, is that trainable?* Jeroen replies; "Yes, it is trainable. By doing it, keep repeating it, repeating it, you can train your eye, of course." *What about that feeling with the horse, is that trainable?* "It's also trainable, yes, of course, but it's easier when you have the talent straight away." *It's easier if you have that talent, but for you it has also improved, right?* "Yes, 100% improved."

When asked to define talent, Maikel van der Vleuten answered, "I think it's a combination of working hard, the **natural instinct in the ring** and **feeling what the horse needs at the right moment**. Being able to read the horse, know what he needs, what he thinks, and being able to always think from your horse's perspective."

As we dive deeper into "talent" in show jumping sport, it becomes clear that the right "feeling for the horse" is very important. Every rider I asked mentioned it. Feeling the horse – what the horse needs and thinks, feeling the rhythm and feeling how to approach the fence. Furthermore, the ability to judge a distance to a jump, or an "eye for the fence," also gets mentioned often. In summary, **the ability to feel what happens underneath** you and the ability to **see your distance to the fence** in front of you are important, if not crucial traits for the show jumping rider. Which, based on my own experience as a show jumping rider, I completely relate to and agree with. Both traits are definitely trainable, even if talent exists and you were not born with these "feeling" and "eye" talents, you can still learn, train and improve them.

Similarly, whatever sport, field or business you are in, figuring out what the core traits are that you need to get to the next level is step number one towards growth and improvement. This will greatly guide your deliberate training, a topic we will explore in detail in the next chapter.

The Equestrian Mixed Mindset

As mentioned in the opening paragraph and from my own experience as well as working with many clients, I have noticed that most often we have adopted a combination of both fixed and growth mindsets. On the one hand, equestrians are generally a very hard-working bunch, so they do believe in effort and hard work. On the other hand, however, as we have just explored, there is this ingrained belief that riders need some natural potential and ability to reach the top in equestrian sports. They can work as much as they like, but if they don't have that natural "feeling," they won't make it. I still hear people comment, "she is really talented" or, "he can't ride." These words insinuate that the rider has the talent they need to succeed, or they don't. Regardless of whether this is true or not, (although we have just read some strong evidence to suggest it's not), how does this "mixed" mindset affect motivation, confidence and grit?

Looking back at my own riding career, I too had adopted a mixed mindset. My fixed belief that I either had what it takes or I didn't, meant that I had developed this incredible need and desire to prove myself. In whatever I did, I wanted to prove to myself and to others that I had what it takes and that I was good enough. My ego-driven need to prove "worthy" of the sport was nothing but a distraction to make things look perfect and get the desired results at horseshows, instead of the focused process of training at home. I was more worried about how things looked on the outside, instead of being focused on the present moment and connection with my horse. I was desperately waiting for a sign that indeed I was gifted and on the right track. Coming out of the ring with a rider's mistake, I would be disappointed, to say the least. I would beat myself up over every mistake, failing to see the twelve or thirteen good jumps and only remembering that one mistake I'd made. Ironically this intense focus on not screwing up meant that whenever I made a mistake on course, I would instantly be distracted and riddled with negative self-talk which would distract me and disrupt my connection with my horse even more, creating an even greater chance of me making more mistakes at the next jumps. As a result, my confidence dropped a little bit more every time and every mistake I made became a sign that I was not good enough. Any negative feedback I got crushed me and consumed me, I could not let it go.

The other side of my mixed mindset believed that if only I worked hard enough, I would make it. Hugely conflicted I went through my day jumping back and forth between these contradictions. With every mistake I made, the belief of not being good enough sank in deeper, yet at the same time, I felt the urge to work harder to have a chance to succeed. As a result, I worked very hard but the harder I worked, the more my motivation would drop. Perhaps this happened because, as Dweck explains, "People with the fixed mindset tell us, "If you have to work hard at something, you must not be good at it. Things come easy to people who are true geniuses." She continues. "The problem with the fixed mindset is that it suggests you either have ability *or* you expend effort. And this is part of the fixed mindset."

Fear of Failure

As you can imagine, the fixed or mixed mindset creates a fear of failure and with that, the urge to be perfect. Being in the fixed mindset meant that I didn't learn from my mistakes and I wasn't focused on improving, only on proving myself. Ironically, I only got more "proof" that I was not good enough. The deeper I spiraled into this fixed (or mixed) mindset, the more I stayed in my comfort zone. More challenge meant more risk of making mistakes and that meant more chances of failure. So, I started to play it safe, going to a training show instead of an important national show or staying home instead of loading the horses up to train somewhere else. We all know we don't grow in our comfort zone, but at the time I had no tools to change it.

Based on this and the theory of some of the Psychologists mentioned in this book (Ericsson and Csikszentmihalyi), I have developed a theory about comfort zones and how the different mindsets influence the amount of risk we are willing to take (Figures 1.1 and 1.2).

Each zone has its benefits. In our comfort zone, we can build or rebuild our confidence. When we are doing what we know and doing it consistently well, our confidence grows but we don't learn or improve as much as we could.

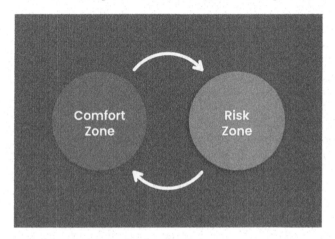

Figure 1.1 Risk taking in fixed mindset.

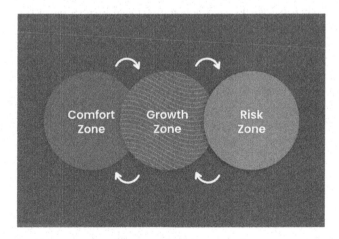

Figure 1.2 Risk taking in growth mindset.

The growth zone is obviously the place to learn new things. When we get out of our comfort zone it's challenging, but within this growth zone, it is realistic to think we can handle this level of difficulty. We have to stretch ourselves to think faster, practice more and grow in new ways in order to meet this new level.

When we push ourselves even further into the risk zone, we really have to rise to the occasion. We may face chaos and failure and we will make mistakes, so we need to dig very deep to stay confident about our abilities, especially when we stay in this zone for a long stretch of time. However, stepping into this risk zone from time to time, as long as it's part of a carefully laid out plan, can be an effective way to find out what we still need to improve and work on in order to get to the next level. That said, it's only recommended when all the other components are in place, such as a confident and experienced horse and having a great team by your side to guide you.

When we are in a fixed mindset, however, two things tend to happen: we quickly move up into the risk zone, only to hide back into the comfort zone at the first sign of failure. In the show jumping sport, one can (unfortunately) enter any class and height we believe to be capable of. The need to prove ourselves and prove that we are good enough often drives us to want to compete at a higher level than we are ready for. As soon as we have one nice clear round we already push ourselves to ride directly at a higher level the next weekend. We want to ride at the highest level as quickly as possible so we constantly push ourselves into the risk zone. Pushing ourselves this way is not part of a long-term view to improve and stretch ourselves, rather a spontaneous decision based on the current results to feel good enough and to get recognition. As a result, we jeopardize our relationship with our horse and their confidence in us as a rider. Finally, after the inevitable chaos that comes with stepping into the high-risk zone, we give up and decide to get back in our comfort zone, sticking to what we know. This often creates a back and forth pattern of moving from the comfort zone to the high-risk zone and back.

As you may expect, when we are in a growth mindset, we love to be in the growth zone, improving ourselves and our horses in a measured, calculated way as well as moving through the other zones to stay confident and to challenge ourselves. Some days staying in the comfort zone to protect our own and our horses' confidence and other days, learning in the growth zone, or even stretching ourselves into the risk zone to really rise to the occasion. The big difference here is that all this is planned ahead of time. There is a plan in place and the type of horseshows and competition levels are carefully matched with the rider's (and horse's) learning level, character and stage in the learning process.

In his book *Peak*, Anders Ericsson,[3] a psychologist I will further introduce in the next chapter, supports the importance of pushing past one's comfort zone. He states, "Recent studies have shown that learning a new skill is much more effective at triggering structural changes in the brain than simply continuing to practice a skill that one has already learned. On the other hand, pushing too hard for too long can lead to burnout and ineffective learning. The brain, like the body, changes most quickly in that sweet spot where it is pushed outside – but not too far outside – its comfort zone."

If only I had known this before, I might have focused more on the process of learning and improving. Asking professionals more questions or even for consistent guidance and support to create a clear growth plan together. I would have been a lot more focused on training deliberately at home instead of trying to prove myself on weekends. Maybe I would have been more excited about training at home and more motivated and confident as a result.

Winning Habit Number 1: The Winning Mindset

Back to the riders I interviewed, we have explored the fixed and growth mindset, now let's explore what their mindset is like. It's hard to say if all the riders I interviewed are 100% in a growth mindset, but what became clear to me, was that they definitely focused a lot of their attention on improvement, learning and asking questions. Many of them mentioned how they often keep thinking about how to improve even the tiniest of details, or when they are not able to figure out what a horse needs, they keep asking and searching until they have found the answer. To me, this is a testament to a growth mindset and I wouldn't be surprised if the skill, to constantly focus on the solution instead of the problem, is a big part of the reason why these riders have become successful. Here are just some examples of a growth mindset at work.

Being Open-Minded and Focused on Learning

Lorenzo, Daniel and Maikel all share their eagerness to grow, learn and improve by watching more experienced riders at work. Lorenzo said, "[I learn] through watching and talking to other riders. I was always hungry to learn from other people that I watched on tv."

Similarly, Daniel's answer really shows us the willingness to, even when not having access to the greats yet, just watch and learn by observing the riders he looked up to. "In the beginning, well, still now sometimes, I loved to go to big shows, national shows as a kid already and watch other people, the famous people at that time in the warm up. How they warm up their horse, how they ride their horse. Of course, over the years, meeting these people, I also talked to them and learned more through asking them questions." Instead of being focused on a lack, he used the resources he had to grow and expand his knowledge. Something we can all do, especially with the incredible amounts of videos and even free material online. Use these resources to get inspired and perhaps even help improve your training.

Maikel Van der Vleuten said, "Even from just watching him [father Eric] or other riders, which I still often do, there's always a lot of things you see and you think that might be something for me to try and add to my own system."

Edwina Tops-Alexander and Piergiorgio Bucci both talk about the importance of dealing with failure in a positive way, turning weaknesses into strengths, which we will explore further in Chapter 5. Edwina says, "Of course I get frustrated when I make mistakes but sometimes it's a reminder for me and it keeps me on my toes. Setbacks actually get me more motivated to improve."

Bucci explains how dealing with failure is a skill he had to acquire; "Now I deal with it [making mistakes] well because of reading certain books and mental coaching. But before, I was terrible, I would be critical and very mean to myself, even if it wasn't my fault. Now, I know mistakes happen so I am prepared and I just want to learn from it so it happens less often or not at all. Also, I learned to laugh at myself more."

In both cases, the riders have made their mindset work for them. They've been open to the idea of growing.

When talking to Jonna Ekberg about her goals, what she loves most about the sport and what success means to her, her love for improvement and growth mindset clearly shone through. She said, "I think, improving myself and the horses – that's success. Of course, I love riding on the team and my dream is to win a Nations Cup one day but for me I think success is working for something and getting somewhere. It doesn't really matter what it is but you are taking the next step forward. Slowly but surely moving in the right direction. That you are improving yourself and your horses, that to me is success. If success was just winning a big grand prix I would feel terrible most of the time, but having a good team that works around you is success and having a boss who is happy with you because he never thought a horse was going to be this good but you made it good, that's success. Success can be winning a Grand Prix or jumping a 6 year old in its first 1.20 m class, it all depends on what is important to you and the context of what you are working toward."

Formerly working at the same stables as Daniel Deusser and Lorenzo de Luca, Jonna was surrounded by other great riders every single day. In a fixed mindset, this could have been intimidating or demotivating to her, but for Jonna it's pure inspiration. "I love the way Daniel rides, I always bother him at home like why do you do this, why do you do that. If you have that mindset like oh I am so talented then you don't work in the same way."

Cian O' Connor's response is similar to Lorenzo, Daniel and Maikel, in that he too is constantly observing others who have mastered specific elements to further improve himself. He shows us how in a growth mindset, there will always be things you want to improve and ways to improve them. "I don't think you ever stand still, you are all the time trying to learn, trying to improve. I look to other people and their operations, how is he/she managing that for where I feel my operation is weaker how could I be better in terms of the amount of business that we do, for example. So we can take a bow and realize we are doing a good job but still strive to do it better."

Finally, Jeroen Dubbeldam portrays crucial elements of the growth mindset by explaining the importance of 1. Having a long-term plan 2. Working on the process and improvement throughout the season instead of the results and 3. Deliberate training and preparation to get specific results. "I focus the whole year on where I want to have a good result. I work on that and I go to shows not busy with winning at that show but instead I'm busy with other things, with little details that I want to improve, that if it comes to the right moment that those points work. Then, when that big moment arrives, I let everything go and then it should be ready. That is how I prepare."

What becomes clear is that our approach to our mindset is a skill that can become a habit with training. For some of the riders above, this positive, growth mindset came easily, but for others, it was something they had to learn and grow into. Luckily, we can all train our minds and grow into a growth mindset.

How to Train our Mindset

On her website, Dweck explains how "Our mindsets exist on a continuum from fixed to growth, and although we'd like to always have a growth mindset, the reality is that we can only be on a journey to a growth mindset. The goal is to recognize fixed mindset elements in ourselves and then reflect on feedback and strategies for how to improve."[4]

In my work as a mental coach, I help athletes become aware of the beliefs that serve them and the ones that don't, I help them recognize where they are on that continuum and how to grow further into a growth mindset. I have noticed over time how sometimes it's easy to believe we are already 100% in a growth mindset. We are doing well, open to learning and working very hard which must mean we are in a growth mindset, right? This may be the case, but as we have learned above, in the mixed mindset, we still hold on to some of the fixed beliefs that are not serving us. Beliefs or thoughts like "I can only enjoy a show or competition when it goes well" or "I'm not sure I should continue, I'm not really good at this" for example. I read *Mindset* quite a few years back, so when I started writing this chapter I decided to take the assessment on Dweck's website again. "Surely I was in the growth mindset," I thought. Turned out that yes, I had indeed acquired more helpful beliefs compared to my riding days, but there was (and is) still room for improvement. The point I'm trying to make is that even for me, a mental coach who has studied Carol Dweck's work, who is constantly thinking about how to help others to think with a growth mindset, I'm not 100% in a growth mindset all the time either. Rather, I'm striving to always learn more and do better. Let's explore three helpful steps to 1. Recognise when fixed beliefs are limiting us 2. Prepare for, and 3. Step into a growth mindset.

Step 1. Awareness

The first step is all about gaining awareness. Not an easy feat, especially when we have subscribed to fixed beliefs for years. By answering the questions below, however, you can assess your beliefs and where you are on that continuum between fixed and growth mindset (at this moment in time). I have taken the online assessment test from Dweck and translated this to (the equestrian) sport. To get a more exact score and clear explanation as to where you are on the spectrum between fixed and growth, I highly recommend you take Dweck's test online (see link in the footnote).

Answering the questions below will give you a first indication and insight into your current mindset. I suggest you answer these questions based on one area in your life as even across different life areas, such as relationships, work, and sport your mindsets may vary. The answers range from Disagree a lot – to Agree a lot (disagree a lot/disagree/disagree a little/agree a little/agree/agree a lot).

1   **No matter how much talent, feeling and eye for the fence you have, you can always change it a good deal.**
2   **You can learn new things, but you cannot really change your basic level of talent, feeling and eye for a fence.**
3   **I like a horse (or sport) most when it makes me think hard.**
4   **I like a competition best when I can do it really well without too much trouble.**
5   **I like work, sport or a horse that I'll learn from even if I make a lot of mistakes.**
6   **I like my work, competition or horse best when I can do (or ride) it perfectly without any mistakes.**
7   **When something is hard, it just makes me want to work more on it, not less.**
8   **To tell the truth, when I work hard, it makes me feel as though I'm not very good or talented.**

Can you tell which statements are more fixed-based and which ones are more growth-inspired? Believing that talent (feeling, eye for the fence, intelligence) is something that can continuously be improved upon, having to think hard, challenge and the enjoyment of learning, are all elements of the growth mindset.

How does this translate to when you are actually on the horse or at the horse-show? Again, the first step is awareness, so the key is to be very honest with yourself and recognize the signs of a fixed mindset. Here are some examples.

Before the event: You mostly focus on results, you may worry about the outcome, worry about making mistakes or failing.

After the event: When the results were not satisfactory, you may be feeling upset, useless, defeated or even like giving up altogether.

Remember to really let go of judging yourself when you do recognize the fixed thoughts and beliefs are taking over. The more you judge yourself for thinking a certain way, the more you stay in a fixed world. Instead, remember that your mindset is just another skill you can train. You want to train your mental skills and mindset just like riding skills, people skills, physical skills, horsemanship skills and other skills you need to succeed.

Step 2. Fixed mindset triggers

The next step is to prepare yourself and to recognize certain situations or moments that trigger a fixed response. Become aware of what your triggers are. When do you fear failure? When do you say to yourself, "now I need to prove myself" or "now I need to do it perfectly"? The more aware you are of your triggers, the faster you can detect your fixed mindset showing up and change it.

Step 3. Ask better questions

Have you ever noticed that when in a fixed "state" you tend to ask questions that make you feel worse? "Why did I do that?," "How could I be so stupid?" or "Will I ever get this right?" Notice how unhelpful questions, lead to unhelpful answers.

The best way to quickly step into a growth mindset is to, instead of trying to get rid of unhelpful thoughts, questions and beliefs (which rarely works), ask questions that trigger learning, improvement and growth. For example, "what can I learn from this?" or "how can this fall, mistake or failure make me stronger, better and faster?"

When creating a new habit of asking helpful questions on a daily basis, we increase our chances of being and staying in a growth mindset even further. Over time, I have come up with three questions I recommend we ask ourselves at the end of every day. These questions trigger a growth mindset and focus on improvement. When creating winning habits, it's all about starting small and focusing on progress over perfection. To start, ask the following three questions at the end of every day. You can then extend that to going through this reflection regime after each class, training and show. The questions are simple:

1 What went well?
2 What could have been better?
3 How am I going to improve this?

Many of my clients keep a notebook in a place where they will easily remember to use it after they are done riding or simply at the end of the day. For some, this may be in the car, for others on your bedside table. The clue to making habits stick is to prepare like a pro. So think about how you will remember to answer these questions. Is there any reason why you might not do it tonight or forget? If so, come up with a plan for how you will prevent that from happening. Have the questions together with pen and paper ready to set yourself up for success and take those few minutes to reflect at the end of the day.

Winning habit # 1 Mindset

- **A fixed mindset** is based on limiting beliefs around your abilities. Believing you either have what it takes or not. You either have the talent needed to succeed, or not. This leads to wanting to prove yourself and often taking mistakes and feedback very personally.
- **A growth mindset** is based on the belief system that anything is possible with the right kind of knowledge, training and action. This triggers a constant focus on improvement and embracing failure as part of the journey.
- **Talent** is a concept that proves difficult to pinpoint. The key skills for a Show jumping rider are; **feeling for the horse** and an **eye for the distance of the fence or obstacle.**
- When competing or learning, keep in mind the three different levels of difficulty. The **comfort zone, growth zone** and **risk zone**. Each zone has its benefits. The comfort zone is great for building confidence, but not for stretching yourself or getting better. The growth zone is ideal for improving in a sustainable way. The risk zone is helpful to test where you are and what you still need to learn, but you (or the horse) risk losing confidence and/or getting injured if staying here for too long.

Notes

1 https://agileleanlife.com/mindset-book-summary/.
2 https://en.wikipedia.org/wiki/Autogenic_training.
3 Excerpts from PEAK: Secrets from the New Science of Expertise by Anders Ericsson and Robert Pool. Copyright © 2016 by K. Anders Ericsson and Robert Pool. Reprinted by permission of Mariner Books, an imprint of HarperCollins Publishers. All rights reserved.
4 https://blog.mindsetworks.com/what-is-my-mindset.

2 Deliberate Training

Time after time, when clients get in touch, they believe their results are the problem. They are inconsistent, winning one weekend and failing the next. Or, they have several "one-down" shows in a row (meaning they have one obstacle down in many or all classes they ride in). They are frustrated and ask me for tools they can use when at the horseshow to fix it. 99% of these issues, however, are not about what they do (or don't do) at the horseshow, these problems originate somewhere else altogether. In order to become more consistent and get the desired results we're after, we must take a step back first, let go of that pressure to "perform in the ring" and pause those expectations around winning.

Instead of focusing on the one (or few) day(s) a week when at the horseshow, let's focus on the training days at home. It's in the training where all the magic happens. It's in the training that we make or break our ride, and not just any training. In order to become consistent or even get to the top of the sport and win championships, we need a crucial ingredient that requires discipline, strategic thinking, lots of repetition, accurate feedback, insatiable hunger for learning (from mistakes), out of the box thinking and out of the comfort zone training, I'm talking about deliberate practice.

According to the late Professor of Psychology at Florida State University Dr. K. Anders Ericsson, a world-renowned peak performance expert with over 40 years of experience researching the subject, it is this deliberate practice that sets the best apart from the rest. Through his extensive research, Ericsson discovered how deliberate practice is a key component to consistent success in any given field. Deliberate practice, as Ericsson calls it, or deliberate training, which I believe is more relevant to equestrian sport, is not merely any training, it is informed, purposeful, focused and well thought out training. In other words, it's deliberate. It is also time-consuming, repetitive and not always much fun. As a result of the deep commitment that deliberate practice requires, we may find ourselves re-luctant to engage with this style of training but as Bob Bowman highlights, Michael Phelps' longtime swimming coach, "Successful people have made a habit of doing things other people aren't willing to do." Deliberate training is an in-volved tool, crucial to become exceptionally good at what you do. This chapter is

DOI: 10.4324/9781003204084-2

about how training can create exceptional performance, how the very best in any given field train and why that's quite different from the approach most of us take. For some of you, this may seem like a radical approach, yet I encourage you to read on regardless. Deliberate training features methods and ideas that can be applied across life skills and it promotes a true understanding of peak performance: applying even just a few elements, can get your training game to the next level. Let's discover together how to create the fundamental building blocks for consistent improvement and how the road to success is not just about working hard, but about working smart.

The DNA Myth

In the previous chapter, we learned about the outdated beliefs around talent and the idea that DNA governs potential. Similarly, for centuries it was assumed that, just like talent, the abilities of the brain to change and grow, were limited. It was believed that one was born with a certain potential and IQ and over time, as one grew older, their brain cells would gradually die not to be restored again. In his 2016 book *Peak*, Ericsson clarifies the history that, "[...] the overall structure of the brain and its various neural networks were fixed. This idea went hand in hand with the belief that individual differences in abilities were due mainly to genetically determined differences in the brain's wiring and that learning was just a way of fulfilling one's genetic potential. One common metaphor depicted the brain as a computer: learning was like loading some data or installing new software — it allowed you to do some things you couldn't do before, but your ultimate performance would always be limited by such things as the number of bytes in your random-access memory (RAM) and the power of your central processing unit (CPU)."

Nothing could be further from the truth. Our brain is absolutely able to change in response to the right training and has the most amazing way of adapting and growing new neural structures and thus expanding its limitless potential. This adaptability of the brain is what Neuroscience calls neuroplasticity. Here is how it works: our brains are made up of billions of neurons. These neurons communicate together through neurotransmitters, firing information from one to the other. When we think a certain thought, move a certain muscle or take a certain action, different neurons fire together simultaneously. When we do this often enough, these neurons that are often fired together start to wire together. This firing together creates a new neural pathway, and in turn, creates a new habit. So when we train a new skill, we create a new road in our brain and when we keep traveling down this new road, just like taking the same route to work every day, this skill becomes second nature and habit. We no longer have to think about this skill and we can focus on the next challenge.

Repeatedly working on the basics, executing a certain movement or jump correctly, again and again, will create an accurate neural pathway, enabling effortless-looking performance. Therefore, in order to create and strengthen a new neural pathway, it's important to not just train to get it right but to train until you can't get it wrong anymore.

Unfortunately, this works both ways. By thinking about how things could go wrong, we strengthen a negative neural pathway. By thinking about how things could go right, we activate and strengthen a more desired neural pathway. Ericsson adds, "The fact that the human brain and body respond to challenges by developing new abilities underlies the effectiveness of purposeful and deliberate practice."

The Power of Visualization

Mental visualization basically means forming or creating a mental image of a situation. This may mean actively thinking about a memory from the past or bringing to life an image or vision for the future. Thinking about a successful performance in the past or imagining the ideal ride in the future, for example.

Accurately thinking about or visualizing a specific performance activates and connects certain neurons, creating a desired neural pathway. Doing this consistently and regularly will strengthen this new neural pathway. With thought alone, we can activate the same neural networks in our brain as when we actually perform the activity. For example, when you move your arm, your brain sends out messages to the muscles in your arm in order to move it. By thinking about or visualizing moving your arm in the same way, you fire those same neurons as if you had actually moved your arm. So by thinking about moving your arm up and down, your muscles will get the signal from the brain and that muscle will grow.[1]

Many studies have been done to prove the effectiveness of visualization in sports. One of which was a study done by Dr. Biasiotto showing how visualization can help athletes. In his study, Dr. Biasiotto asked the first of three different basketball groups to practice free throws (ball in the net) every day for 1 hour. The second group was asked without touching a ball, to only visualize themselves making free throws every day for 1 hour. The last group didn't have to train any specific skill, this was the control group. After 30 days, the three groups were tested. The first group had improved with 24%, the last group hadn't improved, which was to be expected. The second group, however, who had not touched a ball for 30 days but merely visualized the free throws, had improved by 23%! Actively visualizing for 1 hour a day enforced and improved the neural pathways and with that, the physical performance of the non-ball group.

Open any autobiography about a great sports legend and you will learn how they visualized their successes well in advance of achieving them in real life. These athletes dared to imagine the best possible outcome, situations, and performances long before the events took place. Then, weeks, months or even years later their fantasies turned into reality just as they imagined. Take Arnold Schwarzenegger for example, as a young kid in a small town in Austria, he was already visualizing his big and for the time, outrageous dreams. From winning one of the biggest global bodybuilding competitions – Mr. Universe – standing on the pedestal stage, holding the trophy – to moving to America and becoming a well-respected actor.

The most successful and decorated Olympian in history with an astonishing 28 medals, Michael Phelps also trained his mind with visualization every single night. He consistently visualized swimming meets going exactly as he wanted – best-case scenarios, but also the worst-case scenarios to prepare his mind and body for any possible situation and how to respond to that. Like getting water in his goggles, for example, Michael would prepare his mind for when things would not go exactly as planned and visualized exactly how he would respond, over and over again. One infamous example was how he would respond if water got into his goggles during a race. He imagined (and practiced in real life) how he would continue without sight, calm and focused, based on his mental map of the pool alone. On Wednesday August 13, this worst-case scenario became reality. It happened during one of the most important races of his life, the 200 m Fly, which was part of his unthinkable goal, to win eight gold medals during the 2008 Beijing Olympic Games. It was to be Michaels's race, his most competitive stroke, but when diving into the pool that morning, his goggles started to fill with water straight away. In *No Limits,* Phelps explains what happened; "with perhaps 75 meters to go in the race, the cups of the goggles filled entirely." "In the 200 fly, there's a regular and predictable progression of strokes per length of the pool, the number typically going up by one per lap because of the inevitable demands on the body and the fatigue. The first length usually takes sixteen strokes. The second, eighteen; the gap is two because the race starts with a dive. The third length usually goes nineteen strokes. The final length, nineteen or twenty." "Coming down the homestretch, I was just hoping I'd given myself enough of a lead so that nobody could run me down. Seventeen. Eighteen. I could hear the crowd roaring. For me? For someone else? Was it close? Nineteen, twenty. Wall, wall, wall where was that last wall? One more stroke. Give it one more stroke, twenty-one and reach for it, glide just a touch. There, there it was!"

Michael not only managed to swim, blinded, to a gold medal, he also managed to set a new world record at 1.52.03! Even without real-time vision, Phelps' visualizations had provided him with enough practice, creating neural networks to cope with catastrophe to remain calm and focus on his swim. The brain already knew what to do because his training had deliberately dealt with this occurrence.

Similarly, equestrian Olympic champion Nick Skelton admits in his autobiography *Gold,* how he daydreamed about winning the gold medal at the Olympic games in Brazil. "I'd told myself I was going to do it. This began weeks before. I didn't tell anybody else, it was all in my own mind, but I kept going through it, day by day, running through what would happen, visualizing myself on that podium. That was what I was going to do: win gold in Rio with Big Star. Every day I went through it in my head. While I was riding Big Star, working him, I would be going through it. I kept telling myself over and over I was going to win, seeing myself standing on the podium, getting the medal – and how I was going to do it. I jumped every Olympic course I had ever jumped, only in my head, on Big Star. No mistakes, clears, and fast. It was my private vision, no one knew. I totally engulfed myself in Rio and my goal for myself and Big Star: gold." By constantly going over his vision, stepping into it as if he was there, visualizing while feeling Big Star move underneath him, he brought his vision vividly to life. The more we include our senses while in our vision, dream or goal, the more neurons will be activated, creating a powerful message for the brain and body. In Nick's case that message was – there is only one option, to win.

The big difference between just merely daydreaming about your goals occasionally and the visualizing techniques these athletes performed is the consistent practice for at least several weeks, if not months or years and the attention to detail when doing so.

As Nick's example proves, the more detailed these representations become and the more all the senses are included in the visualization, the better. Examples of including the senses are, feeling the horse over the jumps, smelling the showground, seeing the size of the crowd when stepping onto the podium, hearing your national anthem played and tasting the victory champagne. Visualization is about bringing to life scenes in the future as if you are stepping into them now. If, like most of us, you are not yet using visualization on a regular basis, rest assured. Like anything else, with deliberate training we can train our mind and (re) acquire this helpful tool. I will share how to maximize and practice visualization, at the end of this chapter.

Now that we know how to (and that we can) maximize our brain's potential, let's dive into Ericsson's work further and examine the deliberate training of the body.

Becoming the Best

Ericsson reveals in his book *Peak* how becoming the best in any given field requires a different approach and way of thinking compared to merely becoming good at something. He explains;[2] "And here is the key difference between the traditional approach to learning and the purposeful-practice or deliberate-practice approaches: The traditional approach is not designed to challenge homeostasis. It assumes, consciously or not, that learning is all about fulfilling your innate potential and that you can develop a particular skill or ability without getting too far out of your comfort zone. In this view, all that you are doing with practice — indeed, all that you can do — is to reach a fixed potential. With deliberate practice, however, the goal is not just to reach your potential but to build it, to make things possible that were not possible before. This requires challenging homeostasis — getting out of your comfort zone — and forcing your brain or your body to adapt. But once you do this, learning is no longer just a way of fulfilling some genetic destiny; it becomes a way of taking control of your destiny and shaping your potential in ways that you choose."

In order to become an expert, Ericsson lays out a few important, if not crucial traits required to get there. First of all, many experts in sport, music and chess in particular, started young and had the advantage of being stimulated to learn and getting guidance from their parents. That said, Ericsson admits, "While the specific details vary by field, there are relatively few absolute limitations on what is possible for people who begin training as adults. Indeed, the practical limitations – such as the fact that few adults have four to 5 hours a day to devote to deliberate practice – are often more of an issue than any physical or mental limitations." Secondly, what sets the best apart from the rest, is the dedicated time filled with many, many hours of deliberate practice. Malcolm Gladwell famously built upon Ericsson's research to create the 10,000-hour rule, available in *Outliers*.

In summary, investing at least 10 years of deliberate, high-quality training gives you a chance of reaching peak performance and becoming "the best" in your field. But it's the deliberate, highly intentional, and chosen actions that must be at the heart of that training, for peak performance to emerge.

Ericsson clarifies, "With this definition we are drawing a clear distinction between purposeful practice — in which a person tries very hard to push himself or herself to improve — and practice that is both purposeful and informed. In particular, deliberate practice is informed and guided by the best performers' accomplishments and by an understanding of what these expert performers do to excel. Deliberate practice is purposeful practice that knows where it is going and how to get there."

Deliberate Defined

This is a roadmap to acquiring expert level, a journey that takes time, grit and dedication. But once committed to a growth mindset and acknowledging that the journey is as important as the end goal, though hard at times, it is incredibly fulfilling. It's in those moments when we achieve something we never thought we could do, that we find the most joy and excitement.

In order to be accurate and share with you the exact information Ericsson outlined in his book, what will now follow are the exact traits of deliberate practice outlined in *Peak*:

- Deliberate practice develops skills that other people have already figured out how to do and for which effective training techniques have been established. The practice regimen should be designed and overseen by a teacher or coach who is familiar with the abilities of expert performers and with how those abilities can best be developed.

- Deliberate practice takes place outside one's comfort zone and requires a student to constantly try things that are just beyond his or her current abilities. Thus it demands near-maximal effort, which is generally not enjoyable.

- Deliberate practice involves well-defined, specific goals and often involves improving some aspect of the target performance; it is not aimed at some vague overall improvement. Once an overall goal has been set, a teacher or coach will develop a plan for making a series of small changes that will add up to the desired larger change. Improving some aspect of the target performance allows a performer to see that his or her performances have been improved by the training.

- Deliberate practice is deliberate, that is, it requires a person's full attention and conscious actions. It isn't enough to simply follow a teacher's or coach's directions. The student must concentrate on the specific goal for his or her practice activity so that adjustments can be made to control practice.

- Deliberate practice involves feedback and modification of efforts in response to that feedback. Early in the training process much of the feedback will come from the teacher or coach, who will monitor progress, point out problems, and offer ways to address those problems. With time and experience students must learn to monitor themselves, spot mistakes, and adjust accordingly. Such self-monitoring requires effective mental representations.

- Deliberate practice both produces and depends on effective mental representations. Improving performance goes hand in hand with improving mental representations; as one's performance improves, the representations become more detailed and effective, in turn making it possible to improve even more. Mental representations make it possible to monitor how one is doing, both in practice and in actual performance. They show the right way to do something and allow one to notice when doing something wrong and to correct it.

- Deliberate practice nearly always involves building or modifying previously acquired skills by focusing on particular aspects of those skills and working to improve them specifically; over time this step-by-step improvement will eventually lead to expert performance. Because of the way that new skills are built on top of existing skills, it is important for teachers to provide beginners with the correct fundamental skills in order to minimize the chances that the student will have to relearn those fundamental skills later when at a more advanced level.

In summary, a deliberate way of training requires a long-term, step-by-step approach with experienced and knowledgeable guidance to create accurate mind maps and achieve carefully thought out skills and goals. This often means building a life around the training schedule and making sacrifices. In other words, it is an all-consuming, mentally challenging, yet often fulfilling lifestyle of becoming the best version of yourself.

Putting Deliberate into Practice

Let's translate the points above, one by one into more practical steps to improve our training game. It is possible you are already working deliberately toward your goals, but if this approach is new to you and feels intimidating, remember that by just becoming more aware of your current situation and being ready to review your way of training, you have already taken a great first step in your journey. I'm going into detail with deliberate training because it is such an important element of excellence. Even if excellence is not your objective, when focusing more on the process and deliberate training, you'll realize you have more control over your progress and journey than you may have thought.

1   "Deliberate practice develops skills that other people have already figured out how to do and for which effective training techniques have been established." This first trait of deliberate training is pretty straightforward. The equestrian sport has been around for a while and there are many riders who have made it to the top of the different disciplines. As I've interviewed 14 top riders in the show jumping sport, let's use them as great examples of people who have already figured out how to reach the top and that have developed effective training techniques. Generally, whatever it is you'd like to improve in your life, find a strong role model, expert or hero who has already achieved what you'd like to do and study how they did it.

2   Point number two states that; "deliberate practice takes place outside one's comfort zone and requires a student to constantly try things that are just beyond his or her current abilities." I have already shared my thoughts on how the different zones we are in (comfort, growth or risk zone) can strengthen different skills (see chap. 1); however, my examples are more focused on performance at the shows, while Ericsson is more focused on the training at home. So how can we apply this second trait to training more deliberately?

How much time do you currently spend on planning your goals and training goals? Do you plan backward from your goals or are you planning what shows to go to on a weekly or monthly basis? How do you reflect on your shows, do you watch the video? Do you adjust or add exercises in response to the show in order to improve? Deliberate training is about diligently planning, working backward from goals, to improve one skill at a time. Instead of working on the same things every day and working on ten or more skills at the same time, let's look at a more deliberate way of training carefully picked skills that we want to work on.

Let's say, for example, that Jenn has decided that she wants to increase her consistency in the show ring. In order to do so, Jenn and her trainer have determined that the mistakes made, are often related to her ground pace or rhythm when in the ring. On average (roughly 70% of the time) her ground pace is too low, she needs a higher and more consistent rhythm throughout the whole course. To reach this goal, they have determined that Jenn needs to train that "show ring" rhythm more often at home. Jenn has realized that when she is training at home, she has been mostly focused on schooling her horse to close within his body and respond to her aids so he will come back and balance to be able to successfully clear the jumps. As a result, she has not been riding so often in a forward "show ring" rhythm at home. Now that she has realized this, she can begin working on a more deliberate plan to increase her consistency. [By the way, this is something I often work on with my clients, and I remember from my own experience, this actually happens all the time.]

So Jenn and her trainer have come up with a plan. Instead of riding below the "show rhythm" the majority of the training time and only spending about 20% of the time in that forward "show rhythm," she decides to practice that forward rhythm at least 50% of the time when training her horse. This is not just to help her horse to adjust but mostly for her to get used to that feeling of that "ideal" rhythm she needs, to be more in flow and consistent when in the show ring.

Dedicated as she is, Jenn has created a training schedule and she is in her first training session. After a nice warm-up, some walk and trot work, she is ready to get into canter. When picking up her "show rhythm" she feels some (or quite a lot of) discomfort in her body. It feels like she is going too fast and she doesn't feel the same sense of control as she usually has when training at home. Her natural instinct is telling her to slow down, this has been enough forward training for today, but she realizes she has only spent about 10% in this forward rhythm, so she still has some more work to do. She keeps at it and even though she still feels a bit uncomfortable, she stays focused on that "show rhythm" feeling. After a few days of having more than doubled her amount of time in this forward rhythm, she is starting to get more at ease with it, able to breathe normally again and to stay more focused even at this higher pace.

If taking a deliberate approach to training is new to you, this example might seem a bit over-exaggerated. Maybe you've never felt anxious riding at a fast pace, but I know some of you will recognize this feeling. Whether you relate to this example or not, the point is that pushing yourself out of your comfort zone should not just occur at the shows. In fact, the more you face the uncomfortable moments at home and implement tiny, but clear mini-goals positioned outside your comfort zone into your training, the easier things will be when under pressure in a competitive environment.

3   Trait number three is about being very specific when training and working on improving our skills. "Deliberate practice involves well-defined, specific goals and often involves improving some aspect of the target performance." There is a difference between getting on a horse every day and riding for 45–60 minutes versus deliberately working toward detailed and specific goals to improve one specific element in your or your horse's development. Deliberate training means you carefully break down every single detail and element that is required to clear a jump or perform a certain movement. Instead of trying to perfect everything at once, straightness of the horse, the lead change, your position during that lead change and the effectiveness of your outside leg, for example, you just focus on one thing at a time. Looking at Jenn's example again, her aim to improve her overall rhythm on course means she has come up with a step-by-step plan to get there. Together with her trainer, she has determined several exercises she will train in succession to improve her "show rhythm." The first exercise is to increase the time spent in that rhythm, as we discovered above. The second step is to improve how quickly she can get into that rhythm; her aim is to get to three strides from picking up the canter, into "show rhythm." The third exercise will be to hold the "show rhythm" within the turns and on a big circle. Then the next step will be to keep that same rhythm even when making that circle smaller. The horse tends to lose rhythm when in tight turns so learning to keep the same rhythm even on small circles will make tight turns on course, especially in jump-offs, much easier. Each step may take several weeks or longer to train. Only when one element has become consistent and more "comfortable" for horse and rider, will Jenn move onto the next step in the training plan to improve her "show rhythm." Once her target of riding consistently within a "show rhythm" when in the show arena has been met, she can set a new goal of improving another skill or element in her riding.

In order to perform well at a show or competition, thousands of details need to come together. Deliberate training helps to break down performance into those details and then improve them one step at a time. Instead of working on ten different things at the same time making tiny steps of improvement, Ericsson instead suggests we focus on one thing at a time but improving that one element in a profound and lasting way.

4   Similarly to point three, Ericsson recommends that we pay full attention when riding and we must concentrate on what we are doing. I've noticed that when training or riding for many years, especially those who ride many horses a day, when at home riders tend to train on autopilot. They don't have a specific plan before they get on and are just going through the motions. As a result, they get on without really tuning into their

horses and without being fully present. They walk, trot and canter on the right-hand side and on the left and then are done. This is giving the horses their exercise, but it is not deliberate training. It's like driving to work, only to realize we took the wrong exit miles back, or reading a book but not remembering much of what we just read. Compare this to being present while driving consciously and underlining interesting parts of a book while reading it. In the next chapter, we will dive deeper into the importance of focused training and attention.

5   Trait five emphasizes the importance of accurate feedback and the rider's ability to take in, use and come up with their own feedback to improve. This requires a trainers' well-informed and accurate feedback, as well as for the rider to learn how to monitor its own progress in order to adjust the training when needed. "Deliberate practice involves feedback and modifications of effort in response to that feedback." This means a rider needs to be confident enough to make his or her own decisions, both in training and on course. I believe that this decision-making process and independent thinking needs to be trained just like any other skill.

When we grow up learning from our trainers, we are used to following guidance and waiting for instructions. But Ericsson suggests, in order to train deliberately, we must learn to think for ourselves. This concept is as important in training as it is in the show ring where independent decision-making is vital for consistent results. Here is a great example from Lorenzo de Luca who learned the importance of decision-making and the impact that had on his confidence.

At the age of 25, Lorenzo had a sponsor who sent him to ride and train with Olympic rider and coach, Henk Nooren. Apart from riding and management skills, Lorenzo learned an even greater lesson that influenced his career profoundly. Lorenzo explains, "Henk really helps you to trust yourself. For instance, when you walk the course, he will tell you what he thinks, but also tell you, "do what you believe is best [in this line]." By giving me this responsibility, I gained the trust I needed to make my own decisions in the ring and the confidence to know I could do it, even though I was quite inexperienced at that level. In the end, when you ride 3, 4 or 5 star Grand Prix's, being able to trust your own judgment makes all the difference."

Similar to Lorenzo, when I talked to Maikel van der Vleuten, I asked him what happens when he and his dad (who is also his trainer) disagree. In the event that they have a different idea about the plan, which plan does Maikel follow? "We then maybe speak 2 minutes about it and explain why you think it's better on 5 [strides], because then you jump the oxer a bit more forward, because they are already jumping a bit on the back bar there, so then I say "ah yeah, maybe he's right, maybe I should do that."

But as I said, in the end, I am the one who knows my horse best and what is the weak point of the horse for example. If I explain that to my dad, then he also says, "if you stand behind your decision, then go for it." And if it doesn't work out, then it didn't work out. But it's important that you stand behind your decision. Because if you don't believe in that plan 100%, then often it doesn't work."

This wise lesson for both riders and trainers helps us understand the importance of training the mind's ability to make decisions under pressure and daring to think independently. Of course, during the first years of the development of any athlete, listening closely to a trainer and following instructions is very important. However, as independent thinking is a crucial part of becoming a well-rounded athlete, it should be encouraged and become part of the training at some stage in the learning process. It requires a rider to grow and expand its thinking and most importantly, to learn to trust this instinct. This also requires a leveled and mature relationship between student and trainer. In many sports relationships, this evolution occurs. Take, for example, Wayne Rooney and Manchester United manager, Alex Ferguson and Michael Phelps and his lifelong coach Bob Bowman. Both Rooney and Phelps are known to have argued with their coaches and thrown tantrums from time to time, but their relationships allowed both student and trainer to grow together and so successfully evolve. Unfortunately, this evolution can be challenging at times. Here is why:

When we start out as often young, inexperienced riders, we rely on our trainers – they are the experts. In this first phase of our development, we are often in a so-called "child" role (see image below). Our trainers, on the other hand, are often in a "parent" role, telling us what to do, when to do it, and to definitely never challenge their commands. As we continue to grow through our development, it's crucial to learn how to think for ourselves so that when we are on our own in the show ring, we can make decisions in a split second. This requires the students to think for themselves. This is where it gets tricky. If the relationship between student and trainer cannot evolve, if both cannot grow into a new way of working together, the ability for independent thinking and decision making under pressure becomes compromised. What is crucial for a successful and respectful trainer–student relationship is the ability for both to communicate, work and train together in an "adult" way (Figure 2.1).

This requires the student to start thinking for him or herself more often, taking more responsibility for his or her own learning process and career and learning to trust him or herself more. For the trainer, this requires unconditional trust in their student and the education they have provided, as well as creating the freedom for the student to make mistakes so they

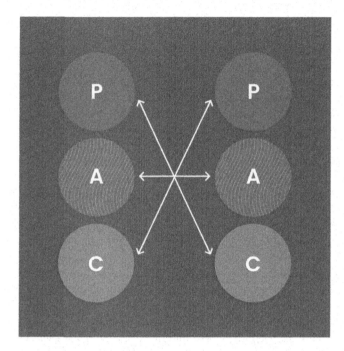

Figure 2.1 Communication roles in training.

can learn from them, just like trainers Henk Nooren and Eric van der Vleuten demonstrated in the examples above.

All three roles serve a purpose but for a successful, long-term relationship between trainer and student, working on an "adult" level is preferable.

6   In trait number six, Ericsson stresses the importance of effective mental representations. These mental representations are best described as mind maps. We all have thousands of mind maps about different people, topics or aspects in our lives. "A mental representation is a mental structure that corresponds to an object, an idea, a collection of information, or anything else, concrete or abstract, that the brain is thinking about." The more deliberately you train, being focused, thinking and reflecting on your training with the help of clear feedback and so on, the more and the more specific mind maps you will create. Starting out as a novice you have very few mind maps. The more experienced you get, however, the more detailed your mind maps will become.

Here is an example of what a mental representation looks like, do you remember the first time you watched a horse go around a jumping course? You saw a series of wooden poles with gaps in between them spread around the arena. None of these jumps meant anything to you or gave you any particular information, they were just jumps. Then the horse entered the arena and you saw a beautiful animal with a rider on top go around the arena and jumping these jumps. Now, assuming you are more experienced, when you look at an arena with jumps, you immediately get more information. You see two jumps in the middle of the arena about two strides apart, a double combination. You see a line that looks like probably a five strides into the corner. The height of the jumps is probably around 1.20 m high. Now, a horse enters the arena and you immediately spot all the tack, note the bit in its mouth and observe the way he is carrying himself, then you look at the rider and notice a great position on the horse, confidence, and the fact she is not wearing any spurs. Within seconds your brain picks up on millions of details, details you might not even be consciously aware that you are noticing anymore. The more experienced you get, the more hours you spend at the barn and the more time you spend in the saddle, the more mental representations or mind maps you will create. You have created mind maps of numerous jumps and how to approach them, of your body position and of all the different movements when asking different things from your horse. You have mind maps from picking up a canter, to shoulder yields, to a lead change, to the position right before takeoff, on the jump, in the landing, the position of your hands, shoulders, upper body, legs and heals and so on. Just for you to be able to stay balanced on a horse while trotting around has required you to learn numerous mental representations and memorize these mind maps to use them again.

This explains why experts can see things going wrong way ahead of time, while the novice has no clue what just happened. Amit Katwala, an award-winning sport and science journalist opens his book *The Athletic Brain,* with a great example of how effective mental representations created one of the greatest goals ever made. Wayne Rooney scored the winning and vital goal for Manchester United on 12 February 2011. "Late in the game, a deflected cross from the right-hand side looped up, just behind where Rooney was waiting in the area. He turned and, with his back to the goal, elected to try the audacious – launching himself into the air to pull off a stunning overhead kick into the top corner. The goal was a triumph of quick thinking and improvization – a goal that owed as much to Rooney's brain as it did to his body. "When a cross comes into the box, there are so many things that go through your mind in a split second, like five or six different things you can do with the ball." Rooney further explains, "You're asking yourself six questions in a split second. Maybe you've got time to bring it down on the chest and shoot, or you have to head it first time. If the defender is there, you've obviously got to hit it first time. If he's farther back, you've got space to take a touch. You get the decision made. Then it's obviously about the execution." Like Michael Phelps' blinded last stretch in the pool, Rooney's extensive mental representations or mind maps, allowed his body to make the right decision and accurately shoot the ball in the net without even seeing or facing the goal.

For equestrian riders, however, it doesn't just end with mind maps about their own performance, they also have thousands of mind maps about how the horses should move, react, behave, jump and so on. Working together and becoming a team with an animal is what makes the equestrian sport so incredibly complex, beautiful and unique. The rider has to always take care of and into account, not just himself as the athlete, but also his equine partner. In training, this means that a rider is never able to focus 100% on himself, which is a challenging aspect of practicing the rider's own skills deliberately for those 10.000 hours. Learning how to ride properly, and becoming a skilled rider takes many, many years of deliberate training. Thankfully, riders can compete to an advanced age compared to other sports. This allows for more time to expand their mental representations and continue to build on their knowledge to achieve excellence. Nick Skelton for example, would have probably retired after breaking his neck in two places 16 years before eventually winning a gold medal in Rio at age 58. Or take "Captain Canada" as Ian Miller is famously called for holding the record of an astonishing ten Olympic appearances. The most by any athlete in any sport so far.

The more we focus on learning, improving and expanding our knowledge, or mind maps, the closer we get to "expert status." Even at the highest level, or should I say, especially at the highest level, the riders I interviewed all talked about how they loved to watch other professional riders warm-up and how they continue learning from others, never getting bored of asking for advice or thinking about how to "crack" the puzzle of their difficult mount. This is why learning from people who have already achieved what you want to achieve is so incredibly important.

7   In this last trait of deliberate practice, Ericsson talks about the step-by-step process of cumulative improvement that leads to expert performance. This process of creating correct mind maps, building one skill on top of another and working in a structured and systematic way toward mastery, requires patience and grit. The road to mastery is not always easy or fun, but being able to embrace the struggle as much as the virtues, is crucial to success. It also requires great teachers who understand the importance of a structured method of teaching, building slowly and in line with the student's learning curve.

I hope it's becoming clear by now that, in order to become an expert, every single choice has a purpose behind it that fits into one of the seven identified traits.

Like we discovered, the equestrian sport is unique in the sense that riders not only have to build and work on their own skills and improvement, but also their horses. Besides their own step-by-step learning process, there is the learning curve of the horse as well. The same principles of building the correct fundamental skills for a great rider apply to the horse. Interestingly, I have noticed that full-time or professional riders often spend a tremendous amount of time thinking about their horses and their progress, but relatively little time thinking about their own process of improving as a rider. Again, this will not apply to every rider, but it may be worth estimating how much time you spend on improving your horse(s) and how much time you spend on improving your own skills. Of course, the sport is changing rapidly and more and more riders are becoming increasingly more aware of the importance of a more holistic approach to their training. Gone are the days (almost anyway) of drinking and partying late and riding early the next day only to win the class. Riders like Kent Farrington, working out at the gym like a true athlete, are leading the way to a new era. An era of equestrian athletes who leave no stone unturned to improve themselves, physically and mentally to maximize their performance and their personal attainment of excellence.

Step-By-Step

What will now follow is the deliberate approach of the riders I interviewed, how they set and work toward their goals and how this translates to a step-by-step process for training their horses. What will become evident is that the same fundamental traits to deliberate training Ericsson outlines (and we explored in detail earlier) are being used by these riders in training their horses.

Daniel Deusser stressed the importance of creating a strong partnership between horse and rider. One that is based on respect and cultivated at home in order to create magic at the most important moments in the show ring. Daniel trains his horses just outside of their comfort zone to create new skills, yet not pushing too far either to make sure the horse stays happy and confident during the process.

"Every day when I train I try to teach them something in such a way that they have respect for me, accept me but also don't lose their motivation. There has to be respect from both sides, I also respect in the end that they are animals. They are not born to only and completely obey us. I think that respect is very important. For example, I'm riding a horse and he bucks or does something he is not really supposed to, I don't always mind it – perhaps it's even good. Because I think if you want to win a class, that kind of self-confidence and attitude, they need to be able to fight for it. It's finding the balance between them being and staying confident and yet having the respect for the rider to follow their instructions. If you school them 100%, their motivation to fight for you might disappear."

Like a trainer with his student, Daniel is demonstrating great awareness of what his horse can handle, what is too much and what is not enough to improve. This requires horsemanship, thus extensive mental representations or mind maps of how the horse learns, as well as his full attention and conscious actions when riding.

This extensive mind map of understanding the way the horse thinks and knowing how to build the horse's confidence, is what separates the exceptional from the very good. Daniel explains how this horsemanship in training, translates to setting step-by-step goals for the shows. Exactly like Ericsson in trait 7, he rightly points out the necessity of building specific skills and working to improve them specifically, never rushing the learning process of the horse, as it would mean having to go back to the fundamentals at a later stage.

"For example, I have Cornet 39 and Tobago, two new horses I have been riding for 3 months now. I know the horses are good but still need some experience, so I set a goal and I train them. You can't always ride to win. Same with these two horses, they are not ready to go full out in a jump off yet, so then I aim to ride a clear round, but then in the jump off I don't take the last risk. I won't go full speed because I feel, if I go really fast I will lose their confidence. I just have to go on the edge of what they can handle. You ride a jump off to give some confidence to the horse and at the same time try to make slightly shorter turns so they get the experience. If you never go faster or take short turns, they will never learn."

Clearly, Daniel is not afraid to continue the training process at a show, being very focused on the process, and yet incredibly successful, supporting the notion that results arise as "a result of" deliberate, process-based training.

"Indeed, one time you go a little slower and then the next time you make the turns a little faster. Or another example, moving these two horses up in height at the shows, it's important to go up step-by-step. So I will start with the 1.50 m on a Friday because it's usually not so big. When your horse jumps well in the Friday class, you can try the Saturday class and if Friday and Saturday classes went well for a couple of weeks (or as long as needed), then you move up again and try the Grand Prix on Sunday."

It's clear that Daniel is the embodiment of deliberate practice, gradually and step-by-step building the skills and confidence the horse needs to reach its full potential. The training schedule per horse is detailed, well thought out in advance, pushing the horse just slightly out of its comfort zone, though never too much, both at home and at the show.

Jonna Ekberg's step-by-step approach to training a horse is to pick your battles and to never solely focus on the horses' weaknesses and at the same time keeping in mind the end goal of being able to ride a clear round. In essence, it comes down to building a relationship with a horse as well as building their confidence.

"I think you shouldn't just focus on the weak points because then you get frustrated. Then in the end you will also take away the good points. I think you need to be a bit selective and just choose what you want to work on and not think 'I need to do this and this and this and this all at once'. For example, I got a horse in the beginning of the year. The balance was really bad and he was very difficult to ride in the ring. Then you take them to the show and you look at what happened. With this one it was always the balance isn't good and the control isn't good enough. The canter is weak, the technique in the backend is not good enough, he can't sit on the hind legs. But I was thinking, when I have the control and can give him enough space in front of the jump then he is going to jump clear. As long as he waits for me I can give him a chance to jump. So for sure you need to improve a lot of things, but you can't do it all at the same time. At the first show, you need to analyze what do I need to jump this horse clear. You have to think. The rider also has to adapt to the horse. If you're at home working on the canter all the time, then you just get angry. You have to first work with the things to help you get a clear round then slowly work with the rest. The rest will also follow. I think it's important to also see the strong points."

Similarly, Maikel van der Vleuten talks about training the horse in a step-by-step way, allowing enough time to build their skills and confidence. Again portraying the importance of horsemanship when it comes to training the horse. "Always try to think from the horse's perspective. If I need to wait two more months to get one step higher, I prefer to wait two and half more months. The horse needs to tell me what he is ready for. Even if you think, I need to make an inside turn to win this class, but the horse is not ready for it, then don't do it. For example, you are working toward a big Grand Prix with a horse. You plan to use maybe four classes to get the horse ready for that Grand Prix. During those four classes I'm really thinking about the way my horse is jumping, the connection with me and the horse, the way I'm riding, I'm just focused on the process of getting the horse ready. Then when the moment is there and you are both ready for it, you work toward getting that specific result and you have to try and be as strong and competitive as possible."

Maikel shows us that even when setting result-based goals, like Daniel, he keeps working on the process of improvement in order to reach those goals. Constantly staying in tune with and training the horses, even at the shows, until they are ready to shine. "It's not that I have to win every class. I try to pick the better class for certain horses and try to work toward that class."

Perhaps, there is no rider more organized and deliberate in his approach as Cian O' Connor. He rightly points out that consistent success is not possible without a clear, step-by-step approach, building strong fundamentals by consistently training the basics. Interestingly, Cian follows Ericsson's seventh trait of deliberate training to a tee. To remind you of Ericsson's words, "It is important for teachers to provide beginners with the correct fundamental skills in order to minimize the chances that the student will have to relearn those fundamental skills later when at a more advanced level." Cian does the exact same thing with both his students and horses.

"I think to succeed in the long run, it's important to have very good basics. For instance, with a horse just arriving at our barn, we will start at the bottom. Let's make sure the horse's feet are good, that he's healthy, that he's fit. Then we would work on the dressage and we would control him. Then we train in-between poles so we have a system, which we would like to bring the horse into. We can move left or right in that system, it's not rigid, we can be flexible. In other words we have a clear system. But if you are a rider and just get on and ride to win a class here or there, that's not success. The most important thing to be consistently successful at the highest level is to have a good basis and to be able to have a structure in the work that you do. You will see people be able to win classes off and on but they never tend to spend 30 years in the top level or succeed at championship or Olympic level because they don't know how to deliver on the big day. You can look at anybody in all different sports. You hear a guy say on that day in 6 months I am going to be ready. Obviously it's harder with horses because they could get a knock in the lorry, or they are lame or a stone bruise or whatever but I honestly believe if you can build up to the big day it's a big help."

Whether training a horse, a student or yourself, deliberate training offers long-term, sustainable success models. Though it may be frustrating at times, long, and time-consuming, it's worth it to really hone in on those basic skills, building, step-by-step a solid foundation for consistent results.

As we learned in the opening paragraph of this chapter, even when preparing for championships of a lifetime, training at home is paramount to success in the ring. Nick Skelton and Jeroen Dubbeldam both decided to stick to this step-by-step approach, working on the basics and "ridebility" of the horse, instead of jumping big jumps to prepare their equine partners in preparation for the Olympics in Rio. Nick didn't jump a five-star Grand Prix with Big Star since he won the Grand Prix in Aachen in 2013. Making sure the horse is not only injury-free but also happy and at its best when traveling halfway across the world is crucial to a successful outcome. At the same time, managing the horse's mental and physical wellbeing while getting enough competition experience is not easy. Luckily, following their own plan and sticking to their step-by-step approach paid of and Big Star was more than ready to take on every track in Rio and bring home the gold medal. Similarly, Jeroen prepared his mount Zenith by honing in on the basics, jumping only up to 1.00 m fences during the last 4 weeks leading up to Rio. This approach might not suit every horse, but the point is that a well-thought-out plan and meticulous preparation, often outdo lots of shows and big jumps.

Hard Work

As we have discovered so far, deliberate training requires putting in many, many hours of hard work. Both McLain Ward and Laura Kraut mentioned how important a strong work ethic is and many other riders I interviewed also emphasized the virtue of working hard. What I've learned through these interviews and working with many athletes, however, is that hard work is a concept open to different interpretations. When McLain works hard, is that the same hard work as you and I put in for example? I've realized we need to be more specific when talking about hard work and what that means exactly because working hard on the wrong thing will not get you ahead. I know a lot of riders who work very hard but do not improve as much as they'd like to or could do. Looking back at my own experience, I know that I worked very, very hard for years, yet my progress stagnated, perhaps even declined over time. One rider might ride eight horses a day but hardly improve over time and stay stuck at the same level. Another rider might only ride two horses a day but keeps improving, gets better horses and moves up on the success ladder consistently. If they both work hard, what is the difference?

I asked Olivier Philippaerts about riding many horses a day and taking time off to rest. His response? "You have to be happy to go riding. If you feel you don't want to go riding, it's better you take a day off and do something different, and then you get motivated again. It's the same if you have a weekend with no show. It makes a big difference sometimes."

Olivier confessed it isn't easy with his busy show schedule to take time off but will seize an opportunity when it arises. "If only on a Monday you take some time off and do something different, that helps. You just need to make a right plan with the people you work with. You tell them you won't be there on Monday or next weekend you have no show and you say, I won't ride I want to do something different. Sometimes you have to let it go a bit because if you ride all day, every day, you get exhausted."

Of course, we do need to keep Olivier's words in context. Professional riders like him work very hard, showing most weekends and starting again on Monday to ride the other horses. Days off, let alone holidays are rare. Within this context, it's important to take moments of rest or time to do something different. Obviously, if you only ride three times a week, taking the day off will not be very effective.

Smart Work

It's time we, just like Olivier, start thinking smart instead of hard work. Smart work is balanced, well thought out and deliberate. Let me explain with an example. Imagine there are two riders, a cowboy and an Indian. They both ride on their beautiful horses for weeks, sometimes months to reach the next village, their goal. At some point, these riders reach a forest. It's hard work getting through this forest and at times they need to get off their horses to cut down plants and trees to be able to continue on their journey. With no map or GPS, they have to rely on their skills and their knowledge of the stars, the moon and the sun to navigate and find their way. The cowboy's approach is to keep working hard, riding for as long as possible during the day, sleeping little and cutting down trees as fast as he can so that he can reach his destination as soon as possible. The Indian has a different approach. He works hard too, riding for long stretches at a time, but he also gives himself and his horse enough time to sleep and recover. He too works hard, cutting down plants and trees to make his way, but he also takes time every other day to climb up into one of the trees, above the forest, so he can see far ahead, making sure he is still on track. It might take a bit of time to do this, but as a result, he stays on track and doesn't get lost. So, who do you believe will get to the next village faster? The hard-working cowboy? Or the smart working Indian?

I was like the cowboy for many years, not taking enough time to rest and recover. As a result, I burned out. I didn't have the mental energy to think of a strategy of how to improve myself and my horses, or how I could get to the next level and reach my goals. Instead, I was doing the same thing, day in and day out hoping for a different result. Obviously, nothing ever changed, largely because I didn't take the time to climb into that tree to make sure I was still on track. The point is that hard work is of course important, but when done without a plan or clear strategy, it is not a certain factor to success. In fact, it might even become an obstacle to success, as physical and mental exhaustion limit the ability to think creatively about improvement and a game plan for success. Functioning in automatic pilot, slaving away and working hard are unlikely to get optimal results, despite your best efforts.

I used to think that, if only I worked hard enough, I would get there. Now I know we need a lot more than just hard work. Instead, when working smart toward your goals you stay focused on what you'd like to achieve yet flexible on how to get there. Yet when working hard, the opposite tends to happen, you are so focused only on doing well at the next horseshow, that you forget to check if you're still on course toward your bigger goals. Ultimately, working smart means you think about the bigger picture. What do you need in order to get to where you want to be? What are all the skills, habits, circumstances and support you need? This way, when you get to the competition, you can just focus on what you need to do at that moment, to succeed.

Rest

Getting to the top in any sport or business is not easy, it's about a lot more than just putting in 10.000 hours. In order to not only get to the top, but also to stay there, continuous learning and deliberate training are crucial. Perhaps the most important thing Ericsson has taught us, is that becoming an exceptional rider asks for much more than just physical labor. Working smart and deliberately toward carefully planned goals, unlike going through your day on autopilot, requires a lot of focus and concentration. Thinking about progress, learning new skills, reflecting on performance, employing creative thinking to find solutions to problems, are all necessary mental skills crucial to deliberate training. This mental work requires huge amounts of the brain's metabolic resources, in other words, it's tiring.

A balanced and sustainable training program, therefore, allows for sufficient rest and sleep to allow the mind and body to restore and grow. This is why extraordinary performers from exceptional musicians to legendary athletes all utilize sleep in order to improve.

Much of Ericsson's work has been based on an important study done to identify what differentiates good performers from the very best. Ericsson studied 30 violin students at the University of Berlin and one of the most important findings of the study was the number of hours the students had devoted to solitary practice. The best violin students had, on average, spent significantly more time on solitary practice than the rest of the violin students had. Unsurprisingly with such intense deliberate practice, they also got more sleep on average and mentioned that getting enough sleep was very important to their improvement.

Another study done with 11 healthy students on the Stanford University men's varsity basketball team, in which they asked the participants to sleep a minimum of 10 hours a night, concluded improvements in specific measures of basketball performance after sleep extension. In other words, by increasing their time asleep, these athletes enhanced their performance on the court.[3]

Recently, research into sleep and its impact on athletes' performance seems to have exploded. Dr. Matthew Walker, a professor in neuroscience and psychology and author of the 2017 bestseller *Why We Sleep,* refers to sleep as a free and legal performance-enhancing drug, without any negative side effects. Another sleep expert, or sleep coach of elite athletes, Nick Littlehales has coached many teams in the art of sleep for performance, such as Manchester United, Chelsea, Real Madrid and Team Sky as well as athletes such as Cristiano Ronaldo, redesigning everything from their sleeping habits to their bedrooms.

With or without a sleeping coach, many professional athletes already get the importance of deliberate rest. Michael Phelps shares in his book *No limits* his exceptional training regime, his eating habits (of an incredible 10.000 calories a day) and his sleeping habits. Michael would always sleep 8 hours and have a 2- to 3-hour afternoon nap. LeBron James has also subscribed to the sleep hack and admits he sleeps 12 hours a night, according to a publication on Livestrong.com.[4] Some of my clients take a nap before important classes and I remember Laura Kraut telling me that Nick [Skelton] used to always take a 20-minute nap in a chair before an important Grand Prix.

For a sport in which mental skills such as clear focus, reaction speed and decision-making under pressure are crucial, good sleeping habits contribute to sustainable and exceptional performance. But let's face it, equestrians are not the type of people who sleep 12 hours a night. Being tough, resilient and hard-working is highly praised and, even though we know sleep is good for us, sleeping for 8 hours a night or, God forbid taking an afternoon nap is often regarded as lazy. Successfully riding and jumping horses requires quick thinking, decision-making, problem-solving and an incredible reaction speed. These are all skills that massively benefit from deep sleep.

We have learned in this chapter the significance of many hours of deliberate training in order to become exceptionally good at what you do. To enhance the benefits of deliberate training, rest should be part of that training regime. When planning that time for rest, it's important to realize that it's not just about sleeping or going on holiday. Sometimes taking a day off to do something different, something that inspires you or catching up with a friend can be more restorative than taking a nap. On other occasions, a nap is all you need.

If not yet convinced, perhaps a helpful way of changing your perception is to ask yourself, "would I ever let my best horse (or friend) work as hard as I do, sleep as little as I do and still expect it to perform well and keep fighting for me in the ring?" Probably not. It is time equestrians start taking themselves more seriously and treat themselves as the professional athletes that they truly are. This means monitoring and adjusting (if needed) sleep, diet, fitness and mental game.

It is important to keep this information within context. Sometimes there is just no other way than putting in an all-nighter or sleeping only a few hours before getting up and ready to compete, and that's ok too. The point I'm trying to make is to live a deliberate life, knowing what works and what doesn't, consciously planning and living your habits and actions as best as you can. When unforeseen circumstances or show schedules impact this planning, it's important to stay focused on what you can control and let go of the "ideal" case scenario.

Another crucial prerequisite for deliberate training is taking time to reflect on what you need to improve and make sure to still be heading in the right direction.

Reflection

A rested mind is much better able to stay focused, calm and positive. It is also easier to come up with creative ideas and solutions. When do you come up with your best ideas? Most people get their best ideas when taking a shower, driving a car, or hand walking their horse. Our brain seems to transform into a creative, problem-solving machine and suddenly remembers things we still need to do. Usually, "working hard" at finding solutions or coming up with a plan doesn't work well. It's when our mind becomes quieter and still, that we can tap into its full potential. As we have learned so far in this chapter, it's the deliberate, thoughtful decisions and plans we make, that help us improve, grow and thrive in the best possible way. In order to do that, we must plan in regular time to reflect on our progress, training and goals. Reflection time is not a luxury, but a necessity for success. The modern equestrian doesn't just reflect on their horse's progress, but also on their own. Reflection and self-awareness are the hallmarks of the successful from sport to business.

Winning Habit Number 2: Deliberate Training

What we have learned so far is that both the brain and the body have a limitless potential to adapt, learn, and improve. Using deliberate training allows you to shape this potential in any way you like, to reach any goal you set, and to do things you were not able to do before. Or like Ericsson says, "[…] learning is no longer just a way of fulfilling some genetic destiny; it becomes a way of taking control of your destiny and shaping your potential in ways you choose."

That is, if your training includes the following; (1) effective training techniques, (2) training outside the comfort zone, (3) well-defined, specific goals, (4) full attention, concentration and conscious actions, (5) correct feedback, modifications of effort and independent thinking, (6) detailed mental representations or mind maps and (7) a step-by-step approach to building skills.

These fundamentals can be applied to training the mind, the body and the horse, creating a lifestyle of consistent and deliberate learning and improvement. Although putting in many hours of focused training outside your comfort zone is challenging, it is also incredibly rewarding. When my clients start to shift into a growth mindset and use a more deliberate approach, they start to focus more on the process (instead of the results) and with that, feel more in control of their destiny. Ironically, many of them find this shift, though hard at times, has made their journey a lot more enjoyable. So let's explore how you too can train more deliberately and feel more fulfilled about your journey.

How to Train Deliberately

In the paragraphs above, *deliberate defined* and *putting deliberate into practice*, we have learned what the fundamental building blocks to deliberate training are and how you can incorporate these building blocks into your training. In addition to that, here follow practical tips to enhance your training game.

1. Get specific feedback

Have someone video your training at home and at shows. You can then evaluate whether what you were feeling at the time corresponds to what you can actually see on the video.

This is also a great way for you to become more aware of your body posture and small details that you want to improve upon. An experienced trainer can also give you invaluable feedback (see next tip).

2. Find a great trainer

Finding a trainer is key to improvement as they are able to provide detailed information and feedback on how to improve your skills. Keep in mind that not every rider is a great teacher. It's important that a trainer is familiar with how top riders think and train and is able to effectively bring that across in their teachings. Ideally, they build a training schedule based on your current experience level and mental game. Also, having a mentor or role model that has already achieved what you want to do can be extremely helpful and motivating.

3. Time alone to practice

When you are always surrounded by other people, you can easily get distracted, making practicing your skills that much harder. Furthermore, practicing new skills requires you to train outside your comfort zone, so making mistakes is inevitable. Being conscious about who is watching could be slowing down your progress. Therefore, plan in time alone to practice. If that's not an option, practice your mental game alone and notice how/if it changes with people around.

4. Get out of your comfort zone

Challenge yourself to train more difficult turns, more technical courses or ride at a higher canter rhythm **at home** to help push your brain and body to this new level (keeping in mind the level and learning curve of your horse).

5. One step at a time

Picking one thing you want to improve on and make a plan for how to get there can be far more effective and actually save you time in learning new skills. Trying to train complex skills all at once will only confuse you (and your horse) and derail your focus. Make sure to create clear process-based sub-goals, pick one or a maximum of two and only work on those until you have mastered them.

6. Try something new

Even with feedback, guidance and focus, you can still hit a plateau in your development, which can discourage you from training hard. If this is the case, try mixing up your training program or try something new altogether, such as training your physical strength in the gym which could help you improve much faster on the horse. Training your mental skills to improve your focus, confidence and positive attitude can also help you to get ahead and stay more motivated along the way.

Deliberate Brain Training

As we have learned in the paragraph above, visualization is a powerful tool to add to your mental skills. There are many ways in which you can use visualization, but here are three ways I recommend training this specific skill.

1. Visualize your best round ever

Especially helpful to boost your confidence and creating powerful and positive neural networks, visualizing and stepping into, your "best round ever" reminds you of how well you have already done in the past. Whether you practice at home or right before you go into the arena at a show, it helps you focus on your strengths instead of on all the things that could go wrong that day.

> Step 1.
> Close your eyes and go back into your memory to that best round you have ever ridden. Go back to feel what you felt then (your horse), hear what you heard then (the bell and music), maybe even smell what you smelled then (that particular horseshow smell).

> Step 2.
> Then ride that course again in your mind as if you are there again. Feel the amazing feeling at the end when you have cleared all the fences and ridden beautifully.

> Step 3.
> Watching videos from well-ridden rounds or wins can obviously help as well.

Here is Jonna Ekberg describing how she uses the visualization technique to get her confidence back when at a show. "I think I have found a way to deal with myself and accept things, to be ok with it and bring out the best. If I start to get nervous, I think maybe one bad thought but then I do my visualization or I watch videos on my phone of a good round, a round I am proud of. The more I train myself to refocus, the quicker the negative thoughts go away. Before it might have taken me 20 minutes to calm down and get into my bubble but now I can do it quickly in a couple of minutes, it has become routine. It's like having a conversation with yourself."

2. Improving a specific skill

The second way of using visualization is by training a specific skill in your mind. Sometimes a bad experience in the past can make us anxious or nervous when repeating the same training exercise. Bad falls, injuries or memories are often a reason for this anxiety. For instance, you have fallen off badly in the past on an oxer or in a combination of jumps, now every time you ride toward an oxer or combination you get slightly tense or scared again. If you would like to work on this without the danger of it happening again, you could visualize doing it repeatedly well and without mistakes.

Step 1.
Start by imagining a comfortable environment, like riding at home for example, or anywhere else that feels safe.

Step 2.
Then imagine practicing that specific skill or new approach over and over again, beginning at the lowest level. So for instance, think of an oxer out of a left turn. The oxer in your mind is so small, it doesn't cause any anxiety and you ride through the turn perfectly, getting your distance easily and creating the perfect jump. Feel how you balance back with your upper body on the jump and being perfectly balanced and ready when you land. Maybe it is hard to imagine at first, but just keep going until you really want to put that jump up.

Step 3.
Repeat in a positive way, until the fear fades away.

Step 4.
Use this particular visualization exercise when you (or your horse) are injured and not able to ride.

3. Visualize your ideal future

Another way of using visualization is by imagining your perfect ride in the future. This looks a lot like your perfect round ever, but instead of it being in the past, you now imagine yourself in the future. We often think about past training or shows and we often think about all the things we did wrong. Instead, imagine your perfect ride.

Step 1.
In preparation for a class or competition, visualize yourself in the warm-up and going around the arena exactly how you would like to ride, confident and focused.

Step 2.
You can also use it to memorize the course plan. After walking the course and watching a few other riders go around (if possible), you finalize your course plan.

Step 3.
Then, you visualize this plan three times, in great detail and exactly how you would like to ride this class. Imagine how that would feel like, what that would look like and how you would ride, how everything would flow naturally and how you make the right decisions before even knowing it.

Step 4.
You can also imagine the prize-giving ceremony and how you will be standing on the stage.

The more you can feel the sensations of riding really well, feeling confident and being connected with your horse, the more powerful this tool will be. Even if the future image doesn't feel very realistic, if you give your brain these pictures of what it is you want exactly, it will pass on the message to your body. Make sure to add these exercises to your training or daily routines to create more consistent results.

Sleeping Habits

If we want to improve our mental power, we need to start with the basics. Like Nick Littlehales says, we can't control the quality of our sleep, while asleep. Instead, we have to prepare for it during the day. If done correctly, sleep is like a legal drug to improve your memory, focus, positivity and ability to stay calm under pressure. Here follow four habits you can incorporate into your bedtime routines.

1. Unwind

Unwind 1 hour before bedtime with small habits that help your body relax after a long day in the saddle and trigger the sleep hormones like Melatonin to do their job. There are so many ways to unwind, find out what works for you. Some ideas are;

1   Taking a hot bath (helps body temperature drop) with Epsom salt, which is great to relax your muscles and to absorb magnesium to soothe aching muscles.

2   Read a book before bedtime and light a candle with your favorite sleeping scent (lavender and chamomile are great ones).

3   Use a few drops of your favorite essential oils to calm the (often overactive) brain and let the body know it's time to go to sleep.

4   Listen to some relaxing music (ideally without using your phone).

2. Routine

Create a clear sleep and wake rhythm for your body by aiming to go to sleep and wake up around or at the same time every day. Planning in seven to 8 hours of sleep a night and potentially a daytime nap of 30–60 min in the early afternoon (Michael Phelps does it).

3. Keep it dark

Back in the day when we didn't have our phones to wake us up, nor clocks, we would wake with the rising of the sun. Light has a great impact on the hormone melatonin that induces sleep and decreases in the morning to help you wake up. Therefore, staring into your phone, tablet or laptop before going to sleep really impacts not only your ability to fall asleep, but also the quality of your sleep. The quality of your sleep is as important (if not more) as the quantity, helping to wake up rested and restored. So leave tech out of the bedroom and keep the bedroom as dark as possible during the night.

4. Keep it cool

One more thing you want to implement into your bedtime routine, which is to keep your bedroom cool. Your body temperature drops during the night so trying to fall asleep in a hot bedroom can make it more challenging to fall and stay asleep.

Winning Habit # 2 Deliberate Training

- Through **visualization, the brain** is able to make new connections and learn new skills, regardless of age or IQ.
- All top athletes use **deliberate training** to improve their skills and performance.
- Deliberate training means; **having effective training techniques, training outside the comfort zone, having well-defined, specific goals, using full attention, concentration and conscious actions.** It also means **getting correct feedback, changing strategy when needed and independent thinking.** Lastly, deliberate training requires **detailed mental representations or mind maps and a step-by-step approach to building skills.**
- In order for a successful and consistent journey, deliberate training should be combined with **time to reflect and rest.**

Notes

1 Brain-muscle pathways have been proven in a study by Brian C. Clark. Clark and colleagues recruited 29 volunteers and wrapped their wrists in surgical casts for an entire month. During this month, half of the volunteers thought about exercising their immobilized wrists. For 11 minutes a day, 5 days a week, they sat completely still and focused their entire mental effort on pretending to flex their muscles. When the casts were removed, the volunteers that did mental exercises had wrist muscles that were two times stronger than those that had done nothing at all (source: http://www.scientificamerican.com/article/how-to-grow-stronger-without-lifting-weights/).
2 Homeostasis according to the dictionary means; the tendency toward a relatively stable equilibrium between interdependent elements, especially as maintained by physiological processes. In other words, when in homeostasis, the physical body is in a balanced state.
3 https://www.ncbi.nlm.nih.gov/pmc/articles/PMC3119836/.
4 https://www.livestrong.com/slideshow/1012209-winning-sleeping-habits-7-pro-athletes/?slide=3

3 Focus

As we have learned in the previous chapter, being focused and concentrated on what you are doing is a crucial part of deliberate training. Whether in competition or in training, without this focused attention, we are easily distracted, thinking about things that are not relevant to that moment and as a result, not tuned in to the most important focal point for the equestrian athlete, the horse. In this chapter, we will explore the third important element to success, a focused mind. In the context of this book, focus means concentrating on one particular point or area of attention. A focused mind is able to zoom in on one or maximum two areas of attention and stay with these focal points for a certain amount of time without getting distracted. As we will discover, in the show ring this means a deep focus on the horse and course plan. In training, this means 100% focus on the horse as well as the rider's own body. Finally, we will explore distraction, how to avoid it and learn how to sharpen our focus with deliberate mental training exercises.

Daniel Goleman an internationally acclaimed psychologist and bestselling author of thirteen books including the international bestseller *Emotional Intelligence*. Goleman has written many books on the brain and behavioral sciences. In his 2013 book *Focus*, Goleman teaches the importance of and how to sharpen our focus in the midst of unprecedented distractions. According to Goleman, and I completely agree, focus is the hidden driver of excellence. He explains how staying focused in the midst of lots of noise or distraction requires selective attention, "the neural capacity to beam in on just one target while ignoring a staggering sea of incoming stimuli, each one a potential focus in itself." In other words, in order for us to stay focused during a busy horse show, we must be able to zoom in on the one thing that we need to think about or do and let go of all distractions, such as worries, negative thoughts, other people watching, and so on.

The Focused Mind

Let's dive a little deeper into our brain and how we focus our attention. Our ability to stay focused under pressure and to shut out distractions is directed by our prefrontal cortex. This structure in our brain is located right behind our forehead

DOI: 10.4324/9781003204084-3

and is able to adapt and change. It is a region of the brain responsible for functional memory and executive decision-making skills and is in direct connection with many other parts and structures of the brain. Its ability to quiet down certain areas of the brain and activate others is the main reason that we can tune in and stay focused on something while still taking in new information. When we are in a state of complete concentration, focused on what we need to do, while still feeling our horse underneath us, our prefrontal cortex is like a conductor in front of an orchestra made up of billions of neurons, creating a beautiful symphony.

We are rarely able to stay 100% focused on one thing for long stretches of time. I myself struggled to focus in school when I was young, but with the help of a mental coach, I really improved my ability to concentrate over time. Knowing how the brain works and how we can train our ability to stay focused, even when under pressure, will give us the competitive advantage we need to get to the next level and succeed whether in business, sport or any other area in life.

Unfortunately, our prefrontal cortex is not ready and fully equipped when we are born. In fact, it is one of the last structures of our brain to develop. That explains why teenagers sometimes struggle to evaluate and adjust their own behavior, as this part of their brain is not yet fully developed. However, as we learned in the previous chapter, our brain is able to grow new neural structures, strengthen certain connections and let go of others. In this way, there are certain activities that help train the prefrontal cortex and help us to quiet down distractions and focus on what's important. These tasks could be reading a book with focus, for example, or performing high executive brain tasks such as coming up with a new plan, writing a report or competing just outside your comfort zone. Anything that requires your full attention and your ability to zone out noises, thoughts or other distractions is basically a prefrontal workout. On the other hand, when we are multi-tasking or managing a busy schedule and constantly having our attention pulled into a million different directions, we are doing the opposite. Though it might not feel like it, multitasking is to the brain, what food binging on the sofa while watching Netflix is to the body. Our brain becomes unfit, undertrained, and learns to be constantly distracted. It's easy to recognize when our body is out of shape, but what about our brain? An unfit brain can be recognized in different ways, such as an inability to remember where we left our keys 2 minutes ago for example, or our focus drifting of constantly.

Why is all of this relevant to riding horses? Well, because unless we already have Clark Kent (or Kent Farrington) like superpowers, we need to train our prefrontal brain so that we can stay focused on our plan, stay connected to our horse and in the moment when competing. When working with my clients, we often work on improving their ability to stay focused. People who are overall considered relaxed and tend to do well under pressure, often have a sharp focus when the pressure is on. Their challenge is to stay focused even when at an (unimportant) training show or at home when no one is watching. For those clients who experience the opposite and get nervous under pressure, we need to work on training the brain to stay focused on what's important instead of getting distracted by overthinking or who is watching. At the end of this chapter, I'll share with you various mental training workouts so you can train your own brain.

Before we do that let's first discover how and why focused attention is so important in training and after in competition.

The Focused Mind in Training

When you're riding at your best and when making great progress with your horse in training, what are you most focused on? Chances are, you're not thinking about that dinner party last night or all the things you still need to do. Instead, when in the saddle, the most important thing is to focus on feeling the horse underneath you. This should get your full attention whether in training or in competition. The information we gather from feeling what is happening below us is what will guide us to what to do next. That requires a strong connection with our horse. A daily exercise I always share with my clients with a view to building a habit is, when they mount their horse to take a moment to really connect with their horse. Just feeling the movement from the horse, or anything else they can pick up on, like the horse's breathing or tension, and so on. In a way, it's like mindfulness for the equestrian rider, being completely present, without judgment, just noticing everything happening in each moment. It sounds simple but if we are in our head a lot or on our phone for that matter, we are constantly either in the past or in the future with our focus. Instead, training ourselves to be 100% present will really enhance our relationship and connection with our equine partner. This means you will notice more details, tiny messages coming from the horse that a distracted mind would not have picked up on. The more feedback and details you notice, the more accurate your decisions can become.

It raises the question: can we stay fully focused and connected to each horse when riding eight, nine, ten or more horses a day? I know many riders who ride this many horses, day in and day out. Perhaps, if you have a well-trained prefrontal cortex you can train this many horses deliberately. However, assuming you ride each horse on average for 45 minutes, riding ten horses a day equals 7.5 hours of full focused attention! I think it's safe to say there is a risk the last few horses will not be trained in a deliberate way, they will merely get exercised. If riding many horses is a deliberate way for you to train outside your comfort zone and improve your riding and focus, great. However, if it's not part of a clear strategy, but merely a way to "work hard" (on autopilot) so you or your horses get better, then think again.

Based in Belgium, the Philippaerts family has a beautiful farm with lots of horses, both for competition (they have four sons who all ride!) and sales. One of the four sons whom I interviewed is Olivier. I asked him about riding many horses a day and his ability to stay focused on all of them.

"I think that is difficult sometimes. If you ride six or seven horses a day, toward the end of the day it gets a little exhausting to stay focused. So I think it's important you ride 1 or 2 horses and take a little break, then ride a few more and so on. But if you ride the last two horses with zero motivation, the concentration is also gone. So when it's enough, it's enough."

In line with our "smart" work approach from the previous chapter, Olivier chooses quality over quantity, which means taking breaks and making sure that when on the horse, he is focused.

"For sure. Some people tell me sometimes 'today I rode ten horses' and I say 'good for you'. I don't think it's good to ride so many horses a day. I would rather ride 6 or 7 and try and do the right thing than ride 10 and do it half as well. In that case, it's better to give some horses to someone else, then to ride just to ride, it doesn't make sense to me. If you're bored of riding that's never a good thing so I think sometimes, it's good when you don't ride for 1 or 2 days and just do something else."

Similar to Olivier, Laura Klaphake makes a point to alternate focused training with taking off the pressure from time to time and relax.

"At home I am not as focused as I am at the show. I think there are some days when I have important training, then for sure I have to focus as much as on the show. That's very important and you have to be focused but then I think you also have to make the difference because some days I just take my horses and I go to the race track for example so then the horse don't have to be so much in the training so the horse can just canter and be happy and I can just have fun and I can think about everything I want to think about. I try to keep the right balance so I keep my horses happy. For sure they have to be focused in the right moment but I think it is important for them to also do something else."

It seems that in order to train deliberately with full focus and attention, we again arrive at the same conclusion as in the previous chapter – we need to find a balance between training our horses and our prefrontal brain and taking moments of deliberate rest.

The Focused Mind in Competition

In Chapter 1, we already explored the two key skills a show jumping rider needs when competing; *Feeling every single movement from the horse* and being able to translate that information. Secondly, we need to be able to *judge the distance to the next jump and so, think ahead*. One point of focus involves the body, feeling, and the other the brain, thinking. This ideally happens all at the same time, which requires our prefrontal cortex to do its job and direct different parts of the brain to focus on these different forms of information.

Laura Kraut described it so well when she said "My focus is probably one of my strong suits, I am able to make quick decisions because I feel what's going on underneath me and I can think about what's going on around me simultaneously. So I will be thinking about what will happen 8 strides away but I am also very aware of what is happening right there underneath me at that moment. For example, if it's a steady 7, I know the second I land going into the line how my horse has jumped that fence, how that is related and how that will impact that 7 strides."

Laura concludes, "Depending on the situation and how I get over the jumps, I can think quickly to rearrange [if needed] because I'm in that moment." In other words, Laura is present, taking in all the information coming at her (from her horse, the environment and the jumps) – which mostly involves the bodily senses (feeling and seeing) and then translating this information into the action she needs to take in order to prepare for the next moment – this mostly involves the brain (quick thinking and decision making) as well as the body's reaction speed. Within a split second, all this information needs to come in through our senses, be processed by the brain and sent back to the body to take a certain action. If other thoughts are entertained even for a second, the speed or accuracy of our actions might be negatively impacted.

During a competition, being able to stay focused in the present moment regardless of the pressure and circumstances, is crucial for quick thinking, observing and correctly processing information and reaction speed. Let's take a closer look at how the top riders reflect on their own abilities to focus and what exactly they focus on when in the show ring.

Most of the riders I interviewed mentioned they are actually more focused when under pressure in the competition ring, a huge advantage when riding into an important Grand Prix. Unfortunately, some of us experience the opposite; when under pressure we get distracted, start to overthink and our mind is all over the place. However, this doesn't mean we can never be pro, it just means we need to learn how to stay focused, no matter the importance or circumstances during a competition. We will look at how to peak under pressure and get into flow in the next chapter.

Edwina Tops-Alexander is very aware of her ability to focus as well as the signs for when she is out of focus. "I'm much better when I compete at the 5-star level. I know I have to be very focused and I have a program that works for me very well to stay focused. I know that if I'm in the ring and I can hear anything outside the ring that I'm not focused enough. This hasn't happened very often but it can. I think it's important to surround yourself with the right people and not to let anything distract you."

To emulate Edwina, you need to; (1) Prepare your mind (and body) before a class to get into your most focused state (again, we will explore how in the next chapter).

(2) Know the signs for when you are distracted, so you can bring back your focus immediately and (3) Have a team of people around you that understand and help you stay focused (instead of distracting you) during important moments.

Similar to Edwina, Daniel Deusser also finds himself most focused when under pressure. "In important classes I never had a problem so far. I have had the situation however where for example, I'm clear and in between I think about how many jumps I still have to go. I have had that in smaller classes. I say to myself, 'come on, focus on the jump', because if you have time to think about these stupid things in between, you are not focused. When you are focused, I think you really ride from fence to fence and you don't realize how many jumps you have left, and I have these courses also."

This riding from fence to fence is a great way to keep the mind in the present moment, instead of thinking about what happened in the past or what may happen ahead.

Laura Klaphake answers in line with the other pros when asked if the pressure has ever undermined her focus; "No actually not, I think I'm always motivated but high-pressure situations like riding for the team make me even more motivated."

I asked Klaphake to walk us through what exactly she will focus on when at a competition. "Well, when I first get on the horse, it's just me and my horse and my trainers. It doesn't matter what's happening at university or with the people around [me], it's just us at that point. Then when I go in the ring, it's more on the course on one hand and the horse and me on the other hand. I am thinking about the course how I should ride the course with this specific horse. I am not thinking about the last training or something like this."

Again, this answer shows the importance of choosing to solely focus on what is going on in that moment, blocking out thoughts that are irrelevant or un-helpful. Trainers and people on the sideline often say "stay focused," which is easier said than done, and unfortunately not very clear. What should one focus on when in one of the most impressive arenas in the world for example?

The annual horseshow in Aachen, Germany is to equestrian sport what Wimbledon is to tennis, one of the most important shows of the year. Riding for her home country as one of the youngest on the German team, the pressure is enormous. I asked Laura to walk us through her routine and what she will focus on when in the competition arena. "First of all, if I am a little nervous it's before the ring, but as soon as I go in the ring it's funny because it's gone all of a sudden. And then, let me think, I go inside and I think about the course again when I finish that I concentrate on my horse. Actually it starts before I go in the ring. Always before I go in the ring I give a kiss to my horse on the neck, it doesn't matter if it is a 1.20 m class or a 1.60 m class. It's my habit for luck you know. Then I go into the ring and I think about the course, when I am finished I talk to my horse quickly. Then we start."

In the case of focus, less is more. Laura's answer reflects the beauty of simplicity and the effectiveness of routines. Always doing the same thing before going in helps the mind to get into the flow (as we will discover in the next chapter). Deeply connecting to the horse should be one of the most important elements in that routine.

Together, Piergiorgio Bucci and I have worked in the past on improving his focus in the ring, especially when at less important shows or classes. Again, the easier the class for these riders, the less focused they tend to be. When I asked Bucci about his ability to stay focused in the ring, he answered, "It depends, it can be a catastrophe and it can also be unbelievable. Normally when I have a really important day or course, or I am riding for the team is when I ride at my best. I need the pressure. I feel the adrenaline and I love this."

I continued to ask what exactly he is focused on when riding at his best. Just like Daniel, PG mentioned, "I focus on one fence at a time." This is such a great way to stay present and really focused on each moment and each jump. Something we can all apply and train our minds to do. Whenever we need to stay very focused and get into the present moment, just like any effective meditation, zoom in and stay with one jump, one stride or one breath at a time.

McLain Ward, just like PG shows us that even the best in the world are not always 100% focused and it's something they keep working on to improve. When asked the same question, how he would describe his focus in the arena, McLain answered, "I would think [it is] at its best now, as well as anybody in the world. But I can be distracted, I can be particularly distracted by noises particularly if the horse is up or distracted as well. For sure I am intense on game day. Something rattles me every once in a while I get a little bit – I have to watch myself a little bit but I would say when it's flowing properly then its strong."

I asked McLain what he does when he experiences distraction and he pointed out one of the most important lessons of this chapter, **the ability to quickly refocus in the moment.** "Well that is when that kind of skill set [that he has learned from his sport psychologist] has helped. You have to catch yourself and pull yourself back to the execution of your plan. For me, that is always my fallback."

Distraction is inevitable, we all get distracted from time to time. What's most important is how we respond to it not just how to avoid it. What often happens is that we get distracted by the distraction. For example, your horse suddenly jumps away or slips on course and you keep thinking about why it happened or how you lost precious time. Oftentimes, our thoughts about what happened are more distracting and time-consuming than the distraction itself and take much longer to bounce back from. Telling someone they should never get distracted is not realistic or helpful. This is the reason I always help my clients train their brains to quickly get back to the point of focus, instead of telling them they can't get distracted in the first place.

McLain teaches us another invaluable lesson. "If [something distracting happens] in the schooling arena, someone crashes next to you or something goes wrong, you just take a quick step back, reset yourself and think about what will help the horse in that moment. Those [distractions] are to some degree, the variables that are out of our control. All that we can control is how we react [to it]. So we have to control our reaction and even if you lose yourself for a moment, don't lose yourself completely. Pull yourself back." In other words, we can't control our environment or what happens to us, but we can control how we respond to it. Staying focused on what we can control instead of what we cannot, is another key part of focus we will explore a little later on.

McLain continues; "Day to day at a competition like here in Wellington, we have a million things going on at once. So we are very organized. I have a great team of people around me and we go over our game plan every night. We know where we are going. For example, you know you are showing say 8–10 horses, three classes per horse, plus we have a stable here. Then we do a lot of business here so you need to see people and this and that. I go back and forth a bit between home and the show. Some days I get here [WEF] at 7 h in the morning and I don't get back till 5 pm. For sure there are days like that but I try to go home a little bit to see what is going on and just to check out for 5 mins." There are many distractions at any given horseshow, so taking small breaks, like McLain does whenever he can, is vital to stay focused when it matters most.

Just like McLain, Cian O'Connor points out the importance of staying organized and well-prepared in advance in order to stay focused when it matters most. When asked how he would describe his ability to stay focused in the show arena, Cian says, "Good, because the course plan we go through is detailed so if the course walk is at 6 o'clock I am not turning up at 6.20, I am there before 6 o'clock. Today I already know the course plan for tomorrow, I saw it on the start list last night and I might even, when I work my horse today, I might even put down some of the lines with poles. Most guys won't know what the course is until they walk in there. So I might emulate some of the lines with poles, I go through the plan in detail, I know good rhythm to one turn inside to two – my horse has a big stride so I can take a stride out to 3 and I go through the plan like a story. So I am not going to go in the ring holding my breath, I go into the ring with a dialogue to myself quietly. I say to my students when I see them coming down to the ring, 'let's go through the plan' and they don't get a chance to be stressed I find. Because they talk through it like a story and from that they relax and they get a clear vision of what they want to execute. I find it really helps to stay focused because it takes the stress out and it lets nothing to chance. It's not like 'oh I wonder how I will jump that', I say make sure you get a big jump there so you can get the 5 strides. Somebody else might say 'see how you jump that and maybe go 5 or 6', well that puts doubts."

Maikel van der Vleuten, very much in line with McLain and Cian, points out the importance of great preparation. By visualizing his course plan and deciding on every stride before going in, he creates a laser-sharp focus for when executing his plan on course. "I completely focus on the plan, the plan I made. When I go into the ring, actually that's too late, I do it in the warm up, when I finish jumping [in the warm up] I always go over the course once or twice. If my dad [Eric van der Vleuten] is there to help he might say, 'listen Michael you have to take care about that fence' or 'the five strides, they ride a bit long', those kind of things. But then I like to visualise the course myself, because in the end you know your horse the best."

Similar to staying focused at the show, at home too Maikel makes sure to be organized and well prepared in order to focus on the horse when training.

Maikel agreed, "That's something that comes quite easily to me. I think it's important to have everything in the stable well organized. I mean, if you are on the horse and you ride the horse for 45 minutes, you have to be able to be concentrated on your horse. I always make a plan, if a horse has been to the show over the weekend, on Monday, I will focus a bit more on the dressage work. You need to make a plan per horse. But to be fair, sometimes when I'm really busy, I'm riding but actually in my mind I'm thinking, 'ah later on I need to do this and I need to do that'. It happens as well, which is normal if you have your own business. But the more organized you are, the less this happens."

I wondered however when Maikel does feel tired or lacks concentration, does he carry on to stick to the original plan, or will he change it to suit his state of mind?

"Normally there are not many things that disturb my plan with the horses. I always try to take my time with my horses. If I only have 15 minutes to ride a horse, I prefer to leave them and let someone else work them. But if you ride, it's as I said, you have to focus on the horse."

Clearly, these riders do everything in their power to maximize their chances of being and staying focused when training and competing. Being focused in the show arena starts by being well prepared, organized and on time at home and in the warm-up. The more we train these controllable traits, the more focused we become as a result. However, some of us, get distracted easily. Let's explore different distractions and how to train our brains to override them.

Distractions

According to Daniel Goleman, we can label distractions as one of two main types: sensory and emotional. The former are all those distractions coming from the outside, like noise from the audience, feeling your horse spooking underneath you or hearing the speaker pronounce your name incorrectly as you enter the arena. Emotional distractions are all those coming from the inside like worrying about what could go wrong on course, negative thoughts about your abilities or how big the jumps are, doubting yourself, questioning if you can do this, overthinking, and the list goes on. Imagine you are at a horseshow for example and your class is starting soon but you have just had an argument with a friend, partner or someone you work with. You know you need to focus but your mind keeps going over the things you said and what he said and how unfair it all seems. This is emotional distraction.

Negative thoughts come up for a reason. Our brain wants to keep us safe. It tries to predict the future based on past experiences, because as long as it knows what's coming, even if very negative, it can try to protect you. However, when at a horseshow and dealing with a 600-kilo heavy horse, those kinds of thoughts are definitely not very helpful.

Apart from negative thoughts, even neutral but irrelevant thoughts can be a distraction. Have you ever found yourself driving to the stables and been completely somewhere else with your mind most of the way? Or ate a whole bowl of cookies without even realizing it? Brushing your teeth, taking a shower or riding your horse, being completely somewhere else with your thoughts? This is called the Automatic Pilot. We are not in the present moment but instead either in the future, past or distracted by our technological devices. How often are you aware of your own thoughts and what you're focused on exactly? If we are not aware that we are distracted by negative thoughts or on autopilot, it will be impossible to change it.

Where Focus Goes, Energy Flows

Self-awareness is incredibly important, as our focus literally shapes our reality. Have you ever walked a course and noticed at some point a difficult element for you or your horse? It could be a water jump your horse might spook at or riding toward a triple combination away from the entrance. At that moment you saw that tricky obstacle or part of the course and you probably thought about what could go wrong. As we think in images, that thought was backed up by an image of your horse stopping at the water jump or you missing the distance. In such moments, we often aim to *not* focus on that and stay positive and so you push the negative thought away. The trouble is unless we replace that image with something else, it is still there. And the more you try to resist that negative thought, the more it persists. As a result, you now ride more tensely toward the obstacle than the rest of the course, you start to maybe pull a bit more than you should, or freeze and don't do much at all. Low and behold, what you imagined would happen, now has materialized and actually happened. Unfortunately, the more we try to push a certain problem away, the more it comes back. Because whatever you focus on, even subconsciously, that's exactly where you're going.

Now, what if we would take this powerful principle and use it to our advantage? Let's take a look at the same example above. You are walking the course and you notice something your horse or you might have difficulties with. You see the image of what could go wrong, but now, instead of pushing it aside, you recognize your fear or apprehension and acknowledge it. Then you ask yourself, "If I don't want that to happen, what do I want?" Often we want the complete opposite to happen. So now you see the image of you clearing the obstacle together. Lastly, but most importantly, you become very detailed in thinking about how, step-by-step you will reach that goal. For example, to clear the water jump you need to sit back after the oxer, pick up the rhythm through the turn, keep your hands a little higher, focus on your offset point and give increasingly more leg during the last three strides. This is just an example, and bear in mind it has been a while since I was in the show ring, so you might approach this a little differently. The point is, that instead of seeing one image of what could go wrong, you have now replaced it with eight images of how you will do it right. This is no guarantee everything will go as planned, but you have definitely increased your chances. You have shifted from focusing on the problem to focusing on a solution.

Being aware of what exactly our mind and thoughts are focused on is crucial to focused attention and so the quality of your training and riding in competition. Once we know what our mind is focused on, we can direct it to stay focused on the things we can actually control and change. All too often we allow our minds to stay distracted on things we can't even change, which takes up a lot of energy, and yet, it changes nothing.

Control the Controllables

The 7 Habits of Highly Effective People has remained a bestseller for over 30 years. Amongst many invaluable lessons outlined in his book, the late Stephen R Covey talked about the importance of staying focused on the things you have full control over and letting go of the things you can't change. Unfortunately, too often we do the opposite. We tend to worry about the weather, the outcome of our performance, who might be watching us or a bad decision we just made on course. Thinking about it won't change the situation and often means losing unnecessary energy in the process, yet letting go is easier said than done.

We all have our worries and concerns such as problems at the barn, situations at home, finances, relationships, our horses and their health and wellbeing, to name a few. Covey explains that the more time and energy we spend on worrying and thinking about these concerns, the more power we give to them and, in turn, the more they seem to grow. The moment we shift our attention, from what we can't do to what we **can** do, we take responsibility and are more likely to take action. With that, we gain control and power. In other words, by

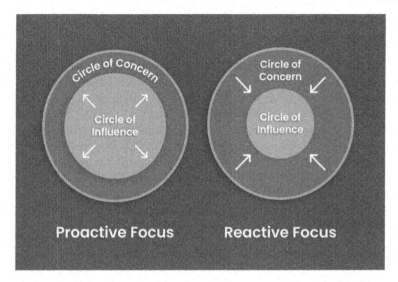

Figure 3.1 Circles of control.

proactively choosing what we focus our attention, energy and time on, we expand our influence (Figure 3.1).

According to Covey, we can categorize people into two categories; reactive and proactive.

Proactive people on the other hand often:
- Focus on strengths
- Focus on solutions
- Focus on opportunities and recourse they *do* have
- Focus on action they **can** take
- Use positive language
- Affect others in a positive way.

Reactive people tend to:
- Focus on weaknesses
- Focus on problems
- Focus on circumstances they have no control over
- Use reactive language
- Get into a "victim" role.

So what do we have full control over? Plain and simple, ourselves, our behavior, decisions, thoughts, habits and actions. By focusing on our own behavior we can reclaim our influence and take more proactive action. Stephen Covey calls this the proactive focus. Expand the circle of influence, and the circle of concern will automatically become smaller. In other words, the more you focus on what you can control, change and improve, the more your worries, negative thoughts and concerns, will fade away. Or as McLain Ward said, you can't control your environment, but you can control how you respond to it.

McLain has worked with Bob Rotella, a Sports Psychologist and author of many mental game-related books, such as *The Golfer's Mind*. One of the most important lessons he has taken from working with Rotella and one he continues to work on is to control the controllables. McLain explains, "I think the things that I apply the most is to really get confident and into my process. How am I going to prepare, how am I going to prepare myself, how am I going to prepare my horse, really controlling the things I can control. I can control my plan for the week, I can control my warm up, I can control my routine, I can control my reactions. Another really big thing that I use is staying in the present. You know how many times I've had a fence down [and] then been the fastest with four [faults and] get a good check?"

In other words, staying focused on what he can control, even when things don't go as planned is something McLain had to learn but, once aware of the importance, he now constantly works on staying focused on the process instead of the results. Ironically, as a result of this awareness and process-based focus, McLain wins more. In fact, he wins more than 30% annually. Obviously, I was intrigued and wanted to know exactly how McLain went from getting distracted easily to staying focused only on what he can control.

"You got to work at it, I find that it's never something you get. I could recite his [Bob Rotella] book to you word for word but it's never something you master. You do it better at times then others. You realize when you're off track a little bit, or your mind is starting to wander to the results or the consequences, you are getting upset or tense because something isn't right. So you keep trying to bring yourself back to it. But I find, for me at least, it's constant [work], it's my biggest struggle."

Goes to show that even the pro's struggle. They too need to continuously work on their skills in order to keep being the best version of themselves.

Winning Habit Number 3: A Focused Mind

We have learned in this and the previous chapter that the quality of our training very much depends upon our ability to stay focused in the present moment. In this skill, the same concepts return and repeat. In order to stay laser-focused on course, you must prepare as best as you can, be organized, focus on the process and on what you can control.

Being able to do all this requires incredible awareness and the ability to catch yourself when you begin to lose focus. Once distracted (which happens to all of us including the ones at the top) beating yourself up or thinking about what happened will only contribute to the distraction. Instead, it's key to immediately get back to the focus point. Think one step at a time, one jump at a time. Only in the present moment are we able to feel the horse moving and fully absorb the big and small messages it's trying to convey.

A focused mind directs our every move (and thought) and luckily we have full control over what we decide to focus on. Being focused means you are aware of what you're paying attention to. If circumstances, distractions or results still govern your focus, in order to maximize each opportunity in the arena, you must train your brain to consciously choose in each moment, what to concentrate on.

How to Train Our Focus

Recently, a client of mine and I were talking about how his focus had increased a lot over the past months. My client gave me examples of how in the past he would notice everyone watching him when he entered the arena and how nowadays he doesn't realize someone he knows has been watching until after he exits the arena. It was something he was very happy about, as it used to be a big distracting factor for him in the past.

Not only has his focus increased, but he has also become more adept at catching himself when distracted and bringing himself back to focus. Ironically, the first step to being able to refocus your attention is to be able to spot that you are distracted in the first place. The sooner you are able to do this, the sooner you can refocus and get back on track. An untrained mind will keep going from one thought to the other or keep getting distracted by different stimuli. So how do we train this wandering mind?

Focus Training

There are many different ways in which we can train our brains more efficiently. Let's explore four ways of focus training together. Meditation, breathing exercises (which are also a form of meditation), reading and other exercises to actively train your brain. Regardless of which method you choose, they all have these two key elements in common:

- You focus on one or maximum two objects only.
- Whenever the mind wanders or gets distracted, you bring it back to its point of focus.

Meditation

One of the best ways to train attention is with meditation. There are many types and forms of meditation and many studies note the benefits of meditating. One of those benefits is a change in brain structure, in particular in the maestro himself – the prefrontal cortex (remember the "conductor" of the brain which we discussed early in the chapter?)

Sara W. Lazar at Harvard University conducted a study in which she compared people who are regular meditators with people who never meditate and found some interesting differences. The grey matter, in the prefrontal lobe especially, was bigger amongst the meditators in comparison to the non-meditators. In other words, practicing meditation helps to strengthen those areas of the brain that help us concentrate and focus better. In another study done by Lazard on meditation and its impact on the brain, the amygdala, the structure of the brain that responds to stressful and dangerous situations, actually decreased in size when the participants meditated often. The more participants reported a reduction in stress perceived, the smaller the amygdala became.

Meditation is not the most commonly used word within equestrian sports (yet), but looking at the research, the benefits of meditation are undeniable and worth exploring.

Breathing Exercise

One form of meditation I personally love and always share with my clients is breathing meditations, although I prefer to call it a breathing exercise. If we are always on the go or on auto-pilot, sitting still and focusing our attention on our breath for 10 minutes can be challenging at first. However, if we focus on 1 day at a time, we will start to feel the benefits and it becomes easier to continue building this habit.

The breathing exercise is two-fold. First, you get comfortable (with a posture that will help you stay focused, like sitting up with a straight yet relaxed back for example). Then breathe in and out while paying attention to your breath. Ideally, you take deep breaths in toward your lower abdomen, you can imagine you have a balloon in your abdomen and are filling it up with air. Then at some point, the second element of the focus training will kick in as you will notice at some point that your mind has wandered off into thought. The only thing you need to do in that same moment is to recognize you are distracted and direct your attention back to your breath. Notice any thoughts of frustration or judgment about your mind wandering, as they too are important to be aware of. However, there is no need to judge. This is what the mind does. We have between 50.000 to 70.000 thoughts a day. Our mind constantly wanders from one thought to the next. Part of this exercise is to strengthen your prefrontal cortex by noticing that you are distracted and bringing your attention back, over and over again.

The days where you feel total bliss when doing this and find it easy to stay focused in the moment are great. But just as great are those days when you need to direct yourself back a million times, as this is what the mental workout is about. Like lifting weights at the gym, you are strengthening your mind.

The reason we breathe deeply into the abdomen is that it helps to create a perfect balance between the body and the mind that we call coherence. When we are stressed or in a fight or flight state, we usually tend to breathe very shallowly, high up in our chest. When stressed for longer periods of time, this short way of breathing becomes a pattern. If we instead wake up every morning and practice for 5–10 minutes to bring that breathing lower into our body and allow ourselves to breath more slowly and deeply, we train our body and mind to get into a coherent state more and more quickly. When trained for a few weeks, we can now start to use this whenever we need to stay more alert, calm, and focused. When riding, the breath can guide us back to the moment and from there we can extend our focus to our horse and the movement beneath us. This helps to stay more connected with our equine partner whenever we are riding. When this too becomes a habit, we will not only be calmer and focused but also more connected to our horse and in the moment when we are at the show.

Here are a few breathing exercises you can incorporate into your day.

Daily Breathing Exercise

1   Sit or lay down in a comfortable position with your right hand on your lower abdomen.
2   Start by breathing deeply in and out two times.
3   Then, just follow your breath deep into your lower abdomen (without forcing it) toward your hand (feel how your hand goes up and down with every in and outflow of your breath).
4   Whenever you find yourself distracted by thoughts or noises, just go back to your breathing.
5   You could imagine your thoughts as if they were clouds; you just observe the clouds as they pass by, and then gently direct your attention back to your breath.
6   It might also help to count every in and outflow of your breath up till ten (if you lose track, start over again).
7   Practice for at least 5 minutes a day and make it part of your daily routine.

Easy Breathing Exercise #1:

1   Breathe in through your nose on a count of four.
2   Hold your breath on a count of seven.
3   Breathe out through your mouth on a count of eight.
4   Repeat four times, twice a day.

Easy Breathing Exercise #2:

1   Breathe in through your nose on a count of five (if five is easy, go up to six or seven).

2   Breathe out through your nose on a count of five (if five is easy, go up to six or seven).

3   Repeat five times, twice a day (or however often you like).

Reading

When I was younger, my ability to concentrate was poor. Whenever I was in the classroom, I would be able to focus for 2 minutes and then my mind would be off as I stared out of the window, daydreaming about my horses. I've realized that reading is a great way of gauging someone's ability to stay focused. In my case, I would get distracted so often that I sometimes had to read the same sentence about eight times before I actually registered the information. This resulted in me always running out of time during exams. Luckily, I started meditating years ago and I have made it part of my everyday lifestyle. Because of that, I have improved my focus to the point that now I can read a full chapter of a book and not get distracted (or not often anyway). So, even when starting out with poor focus skills, with the right training, it can be improved. Jim Kwik is a learning and memory expert, keynote speaker and author. Often referred to as The Brain Coach, Jim has unleashed the brains of many celebrities such as, Oprah Winfrey, Richard Branson, Elon Musk, Will Smith and Bill Clinton, enhancing their memory, reading speed and decision-making skills. Jim himself had a bad head injury in childhood and struggled with learning and reading issues for a long time as a result. At some point, however, he got a great insight that transformed his life. He decided to learn how to focus and improve his ability to learn. Instead of just learning about subjects in school, he made it his life mission to figure out how to learn more efficiently and to retain information more effectively. In his book *Limitless*, he points out that reading is a great technique to improve focus. The whole book is about training the brain, so I highly recommend reading it.

Other Attention Training Exercises

Other ways to train your focus is to apply the same principles I shared above to different tasks. Pick one point of focus and bring your mind back to this focus whenever you get distracted. Some examples are:

1   Place both feet about hip width apart and hold a straight but relaxed posture. Relax your shoulders, bend your knees slightly and now shift your weight to your left foot. Lift your right foot of the ground and place it on the side of your left knee. Hold this position for 2 minutes. Then switch sides. When that is easy you can extend the time or make it more difficult by closing your eyes.

2   Get two tennis (or juggling) balls and hold one in each hand. Now start throwing them over in between hands from your right hand to your left hand. While continuing throwing the balls around, go down on your right knee, followed by the left. Then come back up with the right knee and then

the left so you are standing back straight again. When this becomes easy, change it around. Throw balls from left to right, get down on your left knee first, then the right. Get back up with the left, then the right.

3   Get on top of a big exercise (often called Swiss) ball with your lower legs until you are completely off the ground with your body (shins on the ball). Find your balance and bring your upper body up straight so you can shake someone's hand if they were to stand in front of you. When this is easy, you could throw balls from one hand to the other whilst staying balanced on the big exercise ball.

Apart from training actively with the exercises above, if you apply the same rules of quickly getting back to your focus point, you can use it and train your focus no matter what you do. Obviously riding your horses with full focus and attention also helps train your brain.

The benefit of practicing your focus is that it helps to get into the zone when competing. There are many ways to get into the zone or flow. However, there are also many reasons, often circumstantial, why we usually do not. In the next chapter, I'll explain how flow works and how we can use it to our advantage when needed.

Need more guidance? Make sure to use my online training program (https://annettepaterakis.com/master-your-mind/) for many guided audio exercises and tools including various breathing exercises and morning routines.

Winning Habit # 3 Focus

- **A focused mind** is able to zoom in on one area of attention and stay with this focal point for a certain amount of time without getting distracted.
- **A focused mind in training** is completely focused on feeling the horse moving underneath you and staying focused on the learning process of the horse.
- **A focused mind in competition** is also focused on feeling the horse as well as thinking ahead, judging the distance to the next fence.
- **Everyone faces distractions**, whether **sensory** – from the external world or **emotional** – our internal world. It is not about not getting distracted, its what we do with that distraction that matters.
- **A focused mind is able to quickly recognize its distracted and refocus on the task at hand.** It is also trained to only focus on the desired outcome and on what it can control. In other words, it's able to recognize whether its focal point is helpful or not.

4   Flow

Take a moment to think about your best performance ever, or your most beautiful memory. Chances are, during this special moment you were completely engaged and present, there was little awareness about time and you felt one with your horse, racket or team players. Decisions and reactions came naturally. Perhaps even before consciously thinking about what to do, your body was already doing it. In essence, you found the sweet spot between effort and ease and entered into the zone, also known as flow.

Bottom-Up and Top-Down

Before diving into what flow is and how we can attain it, we again start with the brain and what regions of the brain are important for flow. So far, we have learned about the importance of a focused mind and how our prefrontal cortex is responsible for our ability to stay focused on what we are doing. When thinking about how to deliberately train our horses and ourselves, this focused attention and ability to analyze is especially important. In cognitive science, this way of thinking is referred to as "top-down," as it's the top region of your brain (the prefrontal cortex) that controls and directs the more primal, emotional parts.

However, the lower, older and more primal part of the brain, called the limbic system, has its own important abilities that we can also benefit from. This "bottom up" system works differently and independently from the focused, deliberate top-down system.

In his book *Focus*, Goleman explains these two different systems as follows:

The bottom-up mind is:
- Faster in brain time, operating in milliseconds.
- Involuntary and automatic: always on.
- Intuitive, operating through networks of association.
- Impulsive, driven by emotions.
- The executor of our habitual routines and guide for our actions.
- Manager of our mental models of the world.

DOI: 10.4324/9781003204084-4

By contrast, the top-down mind is:
* Slower.
* Voluntary.
* Effortful.
* The seat of self-control, which can (sometimes) overpower automatic routines and mute emotionally driven impulses.
* Able to learn new models, make new plans, and take charge of our automatic repertoire – to an extent.

The top-down system has the ability to analyze and reflect, focusing our attention on rational decisions instead of emotional reactions. As we explored in the previous chapter, this system is crucial when thinking about how you can still improve, how to train better, or in other words, how you can execute deliberate practice.

However, once you are on the horse, and especially when jumping, you need another way of thinking, we need a faster, intuitive mind that taps into your brain and body's experience, created through thousands of hours of practice. In other words, you need the bottom-up system.

The bottom-up system is constantly checking our environment and getting in large quantities of information through our senses – what we see, feel, hear, etc. It can register all of this information at the same time and, even though we might not be consciously aware of it, it helps select what information we need to focus on at the moment.

Remember Laura Kraut's words in the last chapter? "I am able to make quick decisions because I feel what's going on underneath me and I can think about what's going on around me simultaneously. So I will be thinking about what will happen 8 strides away but I am also very aware of what is happening right there underneath me at that moment."

This requires her to (1) Think quickly, (2) scan many different inputs (what she feels, what she sees, etc.) and (3) make intuitive decisions based on all of this information and accurate mental models. Clearly, what we need in the ring is the bottom-up system to be in charge.

So, what happens when the opposite, top-down system kicks in when competing? As Goleman puts it, it's a recipe for a screw-up. He explains with an example: "Lolo Jones was winning the women's 100-meter hurdles race, on her way to a gold medal at the 2008 Beijing Olympics. In the lead, she was clearing the hurdles with an effortless rhythm – until something went wrong. At first it was very subtle: she had a sense that the hurdles were coming at her too fast. With that, Jones had the thought *Make sure you don't get sloppy with your technique* …. *Make sure your legs are snapping out*. With those thoughts, she overtried, tightening up a bit too much – and hit the ninth hurdle of ten. Jones finished seventh, not first, and collapsed on the track in tears."

Goleman explains: "When she began to think about the details of her technique, instead of just leaving the job to the motor circuits that had practiced these moves to mastery, Jones had shifted from relying on her bottom-up system to interference from the top. Brain studies find that having a champion athlete start pondering technique during a performance offers a sure recipe for a disaster. The motor cortex, which in a well-seasoned athlete has these moves deeply etched in its circuits from thousands of hours of practice, operates best when left alone. When the prefrontal cortex activates and we start thinking about how we're doing, how to do what we're doing – or worse, what *not* to – the brain gives over some control to circuits that know how to think and worry, but not how to deliver the move itself."

In other words, when its' show time and you are in the arena you want to get out of your own way. Instead of the top-down (over)thinking and trying to control or remember every detail, you want to let go and rely on your intuition and experience, or the bottom-up system. You want to be completely present and ride on your feeling.

Intuition and Riding on Your Feeling

It's clear that the moment we start to overthink we tend to mess up, but if we can trust ourselves to ride with an intuitive feeling, we will be in sync with our horse and ride at our best. Perhaps the most important word in this sentence is "trust." It's often a lack of trust, self-belief or confidence that makes us doubt our plan, our abilities or our horse. This might explain why you can ride perfectly well on one horse but make silly mistakes on another. The trust we have in our horses really contributes to us relying on our feeling when in the ring. In the next chapter, I will dive deeper into how we can build confidence from the inside out which, in turn, leads to more trust in our own and our horse's abilities.

No matter what our goals are in life, trust is a very important ingredient to improvement and flow. When we trust ourselves, our abilities and our journey, we have a much bigger chance of not only reaching our full potential and our goals but also to doing that in a more consistent way.

Laura Klaphake explained what riding of your feeling (instead of with your head) really means. She often changes her plan last minute as a result, depending on how her horse jumps each jump, "Lots of the times I change my plan in the ring, cause some distances are mixed and you can easily do 6 or 7 [strides]. We try to make a plan but sometimes, say you plan to do 6 but if you come too deep to the oxer you do 7. Actually it was funny in Barcelona in the nations cup on Saturday there was a difficult line from one oxer I think it was

6 or 7 to the big water then a bending line after very short 7 to a double combination vertical–vertical so it was very difficult. Then we said you should do 7 and 7 and in the end I did 8 and 6. I was clear I don't know why but I did 8 and 6. I had the feeling and it worked out."

Laura describes what it's like when you are riding of your feeling or intuition. It doesn't always make sense, but when completely connected with the horse and trusting your own feeling, following this intuitive decision often pays off.

Similarly, Jonna Ekberg also describes what it's like to connect and ride a horse you don't know at all. Clearly, the best way to get to know your ride is to feel what's happening underneath you. "I like to really get to know the horses. I think I am good at doing that quick enough you know. The first thing when you get on you really feel the horses. When you first get on you need to feel and its like I don't know, you really focus on how it's moving when its over the jump you think 'oh how is it in front how is it behind' there's so much to feel. In the end when you really focus on the horse and try to think every step it takes why is it like this or like that you find their strengths and weaknesses. Then you know how to ride in the ring. It's not easy but I find it interesting and that is something I am always trying to get better. It is an advantage if you can adapt to new horses."

Really feeling what happens underneath you in that way requires complete focus and being present. Really getting into the zone with your horse like that, is the biggest chance of becoming a real team or "one" with your horse.

That said we don't get on the horse with the same frame of mind every single day trusting everything will work out (though it would be wonderful if we did). So how do we shift from a state of fear, worry or overthinking to being in the moment and riding on our intuition? We have to shift from being in our head, thinking to feeling and being in our body. If you're not sure what this means, just pause for a second and shift your attention right now from reading these words to feeling your feet. Feel the soles of your feet, your toes, the temperature in the different parts of your feet and feel any clothes or furniture touching your feet. Now you are focused on your body. Although it's important to think about the course plan and to keep thinking ahead when in the ring, riding the way we planned to ride is something we have to "trust and let happen" instead of control and overthink. When we just focus on one thing that requires our focus to be on our body instead of our rational mind, we tend to do much better. For example, a helpful focus point for show jumping riders is the right rhythm or groundspeed that's needed throughout the course. When focused on feeling that rhythm, everything else comes together too. Or when we focus on our breathing, body position or connection with the horse, we are required to feel, instead of think.

When everything does come together, we are feeling our horse underneath us, feeling the rhythm that we need to ride a fluid course, we are in the moment and simultaneously thinking ahead, we have razor-sharp focus and reaction speed yet our body has reached the right balance between relaxation and excitement. When all this happens at the same time, we are in flow.

The Characteristics of Flow

Back in the 1970s, world-renowned Mihaly Csikszentmihalyi, a Hungarian-American psychologist recognized and named the concept of flow. Together with Susan Jackson, he co-authored the book *Flow in Sports (Champaign, IL: Human Kinetics, 1999)*. In this book, they define flow as a "state of consciousness where one becomes totally absorbed in what one is doing, to the exclusion of all other thoughts and emotions." They add; "Flow is about focus, but more than just focus, flow is a harmonious experience where mind and body are working together effortlessly, leaving the person feeling that something special has just occurred."

"Although winning is important, flow does not depend on it, and flow offers something more than just a successful outcome. This is because flow lifts experience from the ordinary to the optimal, and it is in those moments that we feel truly alive and in tune with what we are doing."

When in flow, we are completely absorbed in the moment, only focused on the process and what we need to do. The result is based in the future so thinking about that tends to distract and disrupt flow. Unless, again, it's about how that result should be achieved, then it's about the process of reaching the desired result. Ironically, by being and staying in a flow state during a performance, the chances of getting a great result become higher as you bring out the best version of yourself and like Csikszentmihalyi says, lift out of the ordinary into the optimal.

From my experience working with many different riders, getting into a flow state before getting on the horse is the best way to not only consistently ride at your best, but also to be most in tune with your horse and your own intuition. When we are not aware of the concept of flow and how to get into flow, we all too often rely on circumstances or factors outside of our control to determine in what "state" we get on the horse. When I mention "state," I mean the physical and mental state we are in. For example, if you wake up "feeling good" you might start your day more positively, approach people and horses differently, get different reactions back and as a result, it might become a good day and therefore, you will ride well. But what happens when you wake up feeling unsure, insecure or downright negative about your performance that day? Or, imagine you are at the show and your horse doesn't feel the same, or the weather is bad or the class has been moved till later and now you don't "feel it" anymore.

Whether performing in sport or in any other area in life, when we are not in charge of what state we get in, the circumstances, other people or our horses will do it for us. Some days might be good, others not so much. When the circumstances or things outside our control dictate how we feel, our riding and with that, our results will be very inconsistent. Instead, getting into a flow state before getting on the horse every time you need to perform means you are much more likely to ride at your best and therefore get more consistent results. Instead of waiting for hindsight to show you that you should have been more focused, or more relaxed or more in tune with your horse or trusting yourself more, we want to make sure we check in with ourselves beforehand, when we can still change something if necessary.

Before we explore how to get into flow when at a show (or training), let's first dive a little deeper into the fundamental components of a mindset in flow according to Mihaly Csikszentmihalyi and Susan Jackson.

1   **Challenge-skills balance.**
2   **Action-awareness merging.**
3   **Clear goals.**
4   **Unambiguous feedback.**
5   **Concentration on the task at hand.**
6   **Sense of control.**
7   **Loss of self-consciousness.**
8   **Transformation of time.**
9   **Autotelic experience.**

Challenge-skills balance

In order to get into a flow state, you want to find a balance between the challenge at hand and your own perceived skills or ability to handle the situation. An important word here is, "perceived." As Henry Ford used to say, whether you believe you can or you can't, you are right. In other words, your actual abilities don't matter so much, it is what you believe you can achieve that matters. Therefore, self-confidence is very helpful for getting into flow.

Go back to Chapter 1 page 23 where I explained the concept of the growth zone and the place where we tend to learn the most. This is the place of optimum challenge-skills balance. This doesn't mean, however, that one can't get into flow when the task is more or less challenging. In those circumstances, it is important to adjust your own goals. For example, when you are out of your league and competing in the "risk zone," you can set different objectives. Instead of aiming to win or get some kind of result, a focus on getting a certain experience can still help you get into flow. Getting way out of your comfort zone is a challenge in itself, so 100% focus on the process is ideal. For example, maintaining the same ground rhythm throughout the whole course or making sure your body is balanced and upright in the landing. Similarly, when the task is easy, setting clear goals can help you stay focused and in flow. For example, in order to get qualified for the grand Prix, I need to ride at least a clear round today and ideally end up in top 25. To reach this goal (even though the end result is not entirely within my control) I will focus on maintaining a forward ground rhythm (as it's a short time allowed) and keeping the horse in the middle of the fences. In the jump-off I will take the inside turn to fence number 5 and leave out a stride toward the last fence. In this way, you create the right balance regardless of the circumstances.

Action-awareness merging

The merging of action and awareness, as Jackson explains it, basically means that instead of the mind looking at the body from the outside, the mind and body fuse into one. Translating this to the equestrian sport, when in flow we tend to be very tuned into our horse, creating a feeling of becoming one with our horse. Some riders describe it as being in their bubble, together with their horse. A great way to connect and become one is to focus on what you feel underneath you whenever you get on. Just feeling the movement underneath you and being completely present to notice the feedback you might get from your horse. For example, what mood is he in today? Does he feel a bit tense or tight? Or more relaxed, cheerful or upbeat? Another way I often guide my clients to become one and tuned into their horse is to imagine light entering from the top of their head and extending all the way to their horses' feet, until they are one big bundle of light. We explored earlier why it is so important to be one with our horse and so getting into a flow state will contribute to that and the smooth, fluent and perhaps even easy feeling of "flowing" through the course.

Clear Goals

As Susan Jackson explains in her book *Flow in Sports*, "goals direct action and focus." I would add however that depending on the type of goals you set, result or process-based, your focus may be directed or distracted. For example, being focused on an end result while riding, such as a clear round, a top placing, or even riding perfectly can actually be distracting and interrupt flow for one and help create more focus for another. Similarly, when thinking too much about what to do while in the competition arena, it can be more distracting and keep you out of flow. Therefore, we apply what we have learned in the previous two chapters. You can prepare and focus your mind with clear (process-based) goals and then, when at the competition, you let go and trust. Choosing a clear focus point when in the ring can be helpful to keep your attention in the present moment and to stay in flow. The more things to "remember" or focus on, the bigger the chance your brain will get distracted. For example, having a clear idea of how you want to warm your horse up in the collecting ring, the different exercises you want to do, what your horse needs to feel like etc. creates more focus. Then, knowing what you will focus on in the ring, such as a clear, detailed course plan and an "anchor" focus phrase like, "forward rhythm" keeps you in the present moment. Being present often leads to more flow. In other words, make sure to prepare in detail (top-down "thinking") in order to be, stay and therefore ride in flow (bottom-up "feeling").

Unambiguous feedback

According to Jackson, "Feedback is critical to successful performance, and athletes who are tuned into the feedback given by their own movements and bodies, as well as by cues in the environment, are able to remain connected with what they are doing and in control of where they are headed." For equestrians this means, the more you are tuned into the feedback you get from your horse and the course, the better you will know what to do next. To be clear, feedback in this context doesn't mean the feedback you get from your trainer, instead it's the feedback you get from your horse, your own body and from the course in that moment. For example, you jump into a line of six short strides, you feel your horse landing far over that first fence, your upper body is still in front of the saddle, and you can see the distance is going to be too short. Based on this feedback within a split second, you decide to ride five strides instead of six. Remember Laura Kraut's words at the beginning of the chapter?

Concentration on the task at hand

Even if we are focused on the process, it can remain challenging to stay 100% focused in the moment and on the task at hand. Distractions, often from our own mind can easily get us out of flow, especially worries about what could go wrong, a bad outcome or what others might think of us. Circumstances can also get us out of focus, such as certain people on the ringside, other horses riding into you in the warm up or suddenly having less time to prepare due to a change in starting time. All of this is distracting and pulls us away from feeling our horse to thinking and getting out of flow. On course, thinking about what just happened, "did that bar just drop or not?" or "why did I just do that?," or thinking about the future, "if only I can ride clear today" or "I can't make any mistakes in this round," all count as distractions. Luckily, our focus is trainable, as we have learned in Chapter 3 and the more we train our ability to stay focused on one single point of focus, the more we train ourselves to do the same while riding.

Sense of control

A sense of control is in essence a perception, a belief about what one is capable of doing. Feeling in control when on a horse or in a difficult course comes from great preparation, deliberate training and a deep inner belief about your own abilities. However, wanting to be in control too much often leads to overthinking and with that, not getting in flow. It's about finding a beautiful balance between controlling the controllables and trusting that everything will work out as you planned. It is the difference between wanting to win really badly, otherwise you can't be happy versus knowing you've got this and you are going to nail it today.

The first is trying to control the situation with pressure, while the second is more trust-based. Ultimately, the only thing you can fully control is yourself, your behavior, your actions and reactions, the way you prepare and what *you* need to do, to get the job done.

Loss of self-consciousness

A loss of self-consciousness doesn't mean falling off and being unconscious, it means that you are totally involved in what you're doing. Instead of consciously analyzing all your actions and questioning, evaluating or judging yourself, you are immersed in the moment, not worried about yourself or your performance. You can trust yourself, your horse and that ultimately everything will be okay. As a result, you're able to ride on your instinct and follow your feeling on the horse.

Transformation of time

"One of the characteristics of being in flow is having a transformed sense of the way time proceeds." Jackson explains. "Generally what is experienced in flow is a shortening of time, so that hours pass by like minutes, or minutes like seconds. The reverse can also occur, with minutes seeming to stretch into luxurious longer periods, providing the perception of having all the time in the world for the actions to be performed." When in flow on course in the show jumping arena, time will most likely seem to slow down, allowing you to react in the best way possible.

Autotelic experience

An autotelic experience basically means that you enjoy what you are doing, that it's intrinsically rewarding. Not because of the outcome or results, but just because of the experience itself. Over time I've learned that when riders focus on the results, they often lose the fun in riding and they can only be happy when they get the desired results or "perfect round." When we focus on having fun and enjoying the ride, the whole experience can be very rewarding, regardless of the outcome. Ironically, having fun often creates great results, as a "result" of you trusting and being in flow.

An example of a flow experience in the show arena could be as follows:

> "I felt great going into the ring. Sure, the course was really challenging, but I felt a deep trust in myself and my horse and I knew we could pull it off. I felt so in tune and connected with my horse, like we were in one big bubble together, only focused on each other and the course. I didn't really think about the clear round my team and I needed to bring home the win. I just focused on one jump at a time. It felt like time was standing still and every decision I had to make just came to me naturally. I didn't notice anything going on outside the ring or even the crowd clapping when I cleared the tricky combination. It was exhilarating to feel so in tune

with my horse and to feel him give his absolute best, like he knew how important this was. It felt amazing!"

Describing his own performance and victory at the Circuit de Barcelona-Catalunya, six-time world champion, British Formula 1 racing driver Lewis Hamilton said, "There is an immense amount of pressure on all of us to perform weekend-in, weekend-out and in the chase for perfection and being in that zone, you can be very, very close but still be slightly out and not be quite in your perfect rhythm. But for whatever reason today, I can't quite pinpoint why, I felt like I was in the most ... It was like a clear zone. The clarity I had when I was driving, I am sure I've had it before but I don't really know how really to get into that zone. Honestly, I felt fantastic in the car. It was physically challenging but in terms of not making any mistakes, delivering lap upon lap upon lap, I was in the perfect zone. And that's the zone I dream of being in. I never would have expected to have a lead of 24 seconds. Even catching traffic, I was gaining time not losing time. There were all these elements perfectly in place. I was very centred in my core and I've got to try to get there every day. I always like to talk about trying to be our higher selves, because each of us has an unlimited capacity. It just felt like I was at a high plane. I am always talking about perfect races and that was one of them. We all try for perfection and it is not always easy to deliver like that but today, for me and the car, I was ecstatic. When I came across the line I didn't realise it was the last lap. I was still going. I was like a horse with blinkers on. I was going to keep going."[1]

Obviously, we always want to be in flow and experience this kind of feeling when entering the arena; however, more often than not, we allow circumstances or negative thoughts to prevent us from getting into flow in the first place. One of the biggest roadblocks to flow is show nerves.

Show Nerves

When looking at the top riders you assume that they have nerves made of steel and that they are as cool as a cucumber when the pressure is on. But listening to these riders talk about pressure, how they view it and if they ever get nervous, their answers might surprise you.

When talking to Olivier Philippaerts about his journey to becoming the confident rider he is today, he explained how in the past, a lack of experience and worrying about what other people would think of his performance would make him nervous. "I got nervous because everything was new so you get stressed because you haven't experienced it yet. With experience it gets better. But when things didn't go well, I wondered what other people thought of that. I don't do that anymore. You should listen to people who train you and are around you and for the rest you shouldn't focus too much on what people say."

I asked Olivier how his parents (who are both experienced riders) guided him in this process. "For sure my father taught me it is important that when you come into the ring, to keep thinking in the ring. Some people, they enter the ring and they freeze and they lose their feeling, they lose everything and the ability to oversee the course. It's important to stay focused in a relaxed way."

Olivier shows us that we don't need to be born with "iron nerves," instead we can all learn to deal with it in a helpful way and as a result become resilient and self-aware, resulting in unwavering mental strength. He continues, "When I was younger, I would get in the ring at a championship and I got nervous. Luckily, I changed that and actually got very good at it over the last 3 or 4 years. I got myself mentally much more under control and I feel the difference now."

Asking Olivier if working with a mental coach contributed to this mental resilience, he replied, "Yes for sure. When I was younger my dad suggested to me and Nicola [brother] to work with a mental coach. I tried a few different people and then I found this guy I liked working with. He really gave me a few techniques, like the way I control my breathing, and I still use them now when I need them. Also through experience, I taught myself."

Digging a little deeper, I asked if this breathing exercise helped him to stay focused in the show ring; "Yes it's very important. For example, if you see great riders like Ludger Beerbaum or Peder Fredericson, you can see they are breathing. When you are stressed, you forget to breathe and you get very tense and you just have to let it go and try to relax and ride."

Although Olivier struggled in the past to keep those show nerves at bay and not let them interfere with his riding, he has learned not only to cope with nerves, he now thrives under pressure. With the help of a mental coach, he learned how to implement simple techniques such as breathing deep into the abdomen and use pressure to his advantage. As we will see, more top riders consciously or subconsciously use breathing techniques to get centered, present and with that, in flow.

Another experienced and resilient rider who admits she still experiences show nerves herself from time to time is Laura Kraut. "Yes, obviously every time you are at a Nations Cup or championship, you are there for your country and you want to do well and you don't want to let other people down. I don't think it is the fear of failure, but it is the apprehension right before you are going in, "I hope I don't screw up." I have worked out a way of dealing with it, I just let it come in and I send it out, I don't listen to it. I either distract myself by talking to someone, or like Saturday night I take the time to focus, I watched 14 rounds and I focused without anyone distracting me and then I walked away and hang out with some people and talked to them. But I don't want to become quiet and let it eat away at me."

In essence, Laura described here how she prepares herself to get into flow; "Yes, I am not a stressy person, but when I start to feel stress I'm easily distracted. So I distract myself and the minute I get on the horse, I relax and am focused. I can be really nervous and get on my horse and be fine."

Even as experienced as Laura is, she still gets nervous, but she is able to do what she needs to do to get into flow. A great misconception is that nervousness means you can't do well. Many athletes fear the butterflies and racing heart and they want to get rid of them. However, as we will see later on, show nerves can be helpful as long as they are not taking over. Remember, flow exists at the sweet spot between effort and ease. Finding the right balance between energy and relaxation, focus and letting go is what helps to reach the state of flow.

Lorenzo De Luca is the most relaxed rider you come across at the show, so I asked him if he has always been this cool under pressure; "No, in the beginning at the first 5 star shows, I was still a little nervous, or actually tense more then nervous. But then you realize after a while that if you are not relaxed, the horses will feel it straight away. Many times we can ride so relaxed and with so much confidence through a big course but then in the jump off you feel a bit more pressure and tense. The small differences, the details can really change the jump. When you realize that, you can change it."

Again, I had to dig a little deeper to figure out how exactly he created this awareness. Was it through watching videos of himself ride? "Yes, but also when you ride, you feel there is something different. In the end, some people might blame it on the horse, but that's the worse thing to do. If a horse jumps so good 1 hour before, why do they change so much [in the jump off]? In the end there is always a reason. And if there is something that changes, of course anything can happen because they are animals, but we need to find a balance between what we are doing on the horses and how they respond. How they receive all this tension."

Lorenzo is clearly very aware and focused on how the horses perceive us as riders. The slightest change in our body language and tension will be perceived by the horse and can impact effective communication. The million-dollar question then becomes, how do we let go of this tension in the moment? Lorenzo's answer sums up the most effective steps to get (back) into flow; 1. become aware of what's happening and get back into the present moment by tuning into your body. 2. Once you are aware there is some tension, relax your body by taking a few deep breaths and 3. Direct your mind back to trust. "Ok when you know it happens, you try to calm down and relax. When I realize I'm a little tense, I will stop for 3, 4 seconds and feel the tension on the shoulders and feel it in my body. In the moment you realize you are tense, you focus on regulating the breathing a little bit and then I will focus 100% on the horse. As soon as I realize there is tension, I know I need to cool down a little bit so I can think about everything again. Then you can relax yourself and trust your horses. Cause when you get to this level and you have the horses for that level, you need to ride with confidence otherwise there is no chance to win the class."

Finally, when Lorenzo is present and in flow again, he can redirect his focus to the horse; "I focus 99% on the horse, I want him to do what I ask, in a good way, without too much pressure. In the end, I really learned how to do this from Henk [Nooren], to get the horse relaxed and how to ride without pressure or tension."

Lorenzo uses the breath to relax, refocus on trust and reconnect with his horse. Again, it's about bringing the awareness back to what you can control and what is ultimately most important in that moment. Remembering to trust yourself and your horse is to the mind, what deep breathing is to the body. Combined, it's a powerful way to quickly get back in flow.

In line with the other riders, Daniel Deusser had to learn through experience and find his way to confidence. "I think confidence comes with experience. For sure, I did not always have it. I remember for example, when I was a young rider, I had a very good result in the German championships and so I was qualified to go to CSIO Aachen for the first time in my career. Being in Aachen the first time, having a good or a bad result was a totally different world. Now when I go to Aachen I know what is expected of me. But, for sure, the first times in Aachen I was more nervous than riding the Grand Prix in Aachen now."

"I think if you know what is expected of you, you can train for it at home. Of course, it can still go wrong but at least you are prepared, you cannot do more than that. Like, you cannot do more than the other [riders], the other ones do the same. If you have a good horse and you train well, there's no reason to be nervous."

Jonna Ekberg and I have worked together in the past on staying consistent no matter the circumstances. Jonna too has experienced how show nerves can block getting into flow, but she has learned to use them to her advantage. "I think now it's a lot better, I have learned how to deal with it in another way. I like the breathing exercise that comes automatically for me now, to take a deep breath or to get the pulse down a bit. I think also I have learned to accept that it is okay to be nervous, it doesn't have to be a bad thing. You can make something positive out of it. In the end when you get a bit tense walking the course it's not because you are stupid or anything, it's because you want to do so well. I have learned to accept the fact I get nervous because I want to do well, I want to win this class. Or in a Nations Cup with a team it's so different, the atmosphere, it has been a different situation for me the last 2 years. I think I have found a better way to deal with myself and accept things, to be okay with the nerves and bring out the best. When I start getting nervous, I now maybe only have one bad thought. Then I will visualize the course and then I always have videos in my phone, so I can quickly look at a good round, a round I am proud of. The more I do this routine, the quicker the nervous feeling goes away. Before it might take me 20 minutes to calm down and get in my bubble but now I can do it quickly in a couple of minutes, it's all routine. It's like having a conversation with yourself."[2]

What about McLain Ward? No way he ever gets nervous, right? Think again; "I mean I think it's a little bit better but yes I get nervous. I think when you stop getting a bit nervous the end is near, you know. You don't care anymore, right? You deal with it better, you handle it better, I'm less gutted about what maybe somebody else thinks if I have a bad day. It still bothers me a bit, but it's not like I can't show my face the next day."

If you thought you are the only one who gets nervous, you thought wrong. Even at the highest level, riders do get nervous. However, they have clearly found a way to deal with it and many mention that the moment they get on the horse, they are completely focused.

The biggest reason why we don't get into a flow state or don't manage to stay in it when riding is because of a lack of trust. Whether we don't trust ourselves, our ability to stay cool under pressure, our horses or that the outcome will be as desired, this lack of trust often results in the activation of the fight or flight system. This in turn activates more distracting thoughts and worries. When we allow our survival brain to take over, it will most likely prevent us from getting into flow and therefore ride at our best. This also explains why, when preparing for a competition, being focused on, or worse − getting feedback from your trainer on − what not to do, is recipe for disaster.

So how do we avoid this from happening? How do we stay in control and, nervous or not, get into a flow state? Yet again, the key lies in understanding how our brain works.

The Brain Under Pressure

What happens when you feel nervous? Your heart races in your chest, your legs are all shaky, butterflies in your tummy or feeling sick. Your hands, arms and shoulders are tense, which makes you come out of your seat more than you want. This in turn leads to you not seeing the distance to the jumps the same way and losing the connection with your horse. These are all signs that your brain's survival system has kicked in.

The brain is like a control center of the body. All the information that comes in through the senses will be checked there first. Within the center of our brain, there is a part called the limbic system. The main focus of this limbic system is to keep us alive and warn us in case of any danger. In particular a small, almond-shaped structure in the center of this primal part of the brain, which is called the amygdala. All the information that enters through our senses; what we hear, see, feel, smell and taste, goes directly to this amygdala. Like a lighthouse, the amygdala is constantly screening every situation to determine whether it's safe or not. If there is no danger, you just carry on, but if there is even the slightest chance the situation you are in, might, potentially be dangerous for you, a whole process starts in your body preparing you to either fight or run away. At that moment, this fight or flight response will signal your adrenal glands to release hormones like adrenaline and cortisol (the latter being a stress hormone). This in turn leads to a chain reaction of changes in the body that help tap into every inch of energy and strength the body has to survive.

When under pressure, the limbic system takes over control from the "rational" Neocortex, the top part of the brain we learned about in the last chapter, as rational thinking could compromise the chances of survival (contemplating which escape route to take while being chased by a bear, might slow you down and get you killed). This means that normal, rational thinking becomes compromised.

Have you ever experienced suddenly forgetting everything you learned or forgetting your course plan? Perhaps you stopped counting your strides or just stopped riding? This is because the limbic system hijacked your Neocortex and you simply couldn't "think" anymore.

This process explains why, when under pressure, your "nerves" are hijacking your ride and you are not able to ride like you usually do, think clearly or stay connected with your horse. The good news is that you can train your brain to react differently. As the limbic system is directly connected to the heart, changing your heart-rate helps to deactivate the "brain block" and instead, access rational thinking again more easily.

As we learned in the previous chapter, breathing low and slow and with that, relaxing the body helps to send a signal to the brain saying, "I'm safe." However, because this survival system has been around for thousands of years and has been crucial to our survival, just taking a few deep breaths when you need it, might not be enough to override the fight or flight. Therefore, training the brain and body to react differently to high-pressure situations is key to staying focused and getting into flow.

Winning Habit Number 4: Flow

In an ideal world, we would always be in our own bubble, completely focused at the task at hand and nothing would be able to distract us, not even our own thoughts. Unfortunately, this is not always the case. To better understand how we can be and stay in our zone or in flow, we must first better understand how flow works.

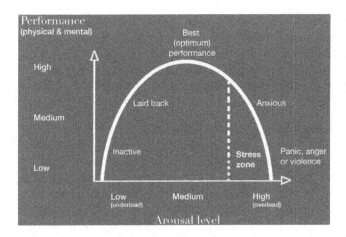

Figure 4.1 Pressure and performance graph.

The way we get into flow is very personal and it strongly depends on how we deal with pressure and stressful situations. When we understand how we respond to pressure, we can also better understand how we get into our bubble, zone or a flow state. As you can see in the image below, performing under pressure follows a bell-shaped curve. Two psychologists Robert M. Yerkes and John Dillingham Dodson studied the relationship between pressure and performance and in 1908 developed the Yerkes-Dodson law. According to this law, performance increases with mental and physical arousal, but only up to a certain point, when the pressure becomes too high, performance decreases. In other words, everybody needs pressure to perform well, but the amount of pressure depends on the task and on you as a person. This process is best illustrated with the inverted U-curve.

When the pressure goes up, performance goes up. However, there is a tipping point. At the top of the curve, we are in flow. When we go over the tipping point, we crack under the pressure and easily get nervous, anxious, angry or stressed (Figure 4.1).

Generally, we can divide people into two groups. Those in the first group are naturally laid-back, they tend to be more relaxed. They might be late sometimes when preparing or getting to a show or in training and they can be in their own little world sometimes. They tend to do better or even thrive under pressure, so Grand Prix day is the day they generally ride at their best. As a result, they might get bored or lose focus when at a small or "unimportant" training (show). In other words, they need some (or a lot of) pressure (more accurately – arousal) to perform well. People in this group can also feel nervous at times but as a general rule they tend to do well under pressure, even when the stakes are high.

On the other hand, there are the riders in the second group who tend to get nervous more easily, distracted quickly and get into a fight, flight (or freeze) mode when competing, or perhaps even just by thinking of the upcoming show. They make mistakes in the ring that they would normally never make at home, not because they aren't focused enough, but because they want it so badly and put too much pressure on themselves. In contrast to the first group, this group needs relaxation to get back to their flow state.

From talking to the riders during the interviews, I got the impression that many, if not all of them, tend to do better under pressure. They thrive when the pressure is on and they have to make it happen. They have therefore managed to seize the opportunities that have come their way. Although many of these riders have naturally found their way to get into their zone when under pressure, getting into a flow state is something we can all learn how to do within minutes, sometimes even seconds. It all comes down to our preparation, so of course I was curious about the way top riders prepare before they go into the show ring. Although many answered that they didn't have a set routine, after they took a moment to think about it, they often realized that actually there were a few things they always did, probably so routinely, that they didn't even realize they too had a routine to get into flow.

How the Best Get Into Flow

We all know prevention is better than cure. Similarly, it's much more effective to prepare yourself mentally before getting on than having to solve or intervene when distracted while riding.

We already learned above how Lorenzo De Luca has found an effective way to get back to flow when already on the horse, but he also knows how important preparation is and how just a few small but significant actions combined can create a powerful routine and thus a harmonious ride; "I stretch myself because I want my body to respond the way I want, and I make sure my horses are happy. Have a good sleep at night. Make sure I'm not late."

Piergiorgio Bucci and I also worked together on creating a helpful prep routine to get focused and in flow; "Before I go on the horse, I sit and breathe into my stomach and I check if I am nervous. I can't remember a time when I was too nervous, usually I'm too relaxed. So I move my legs, I listen to music. It comes quickly. Then I visualise the course three times, then I'm ready to go. I used to visualise but I realised I wasn't visualising until the end of the course. I needed to consciously visualise the entire course. Sometimes I am too excited to jump the last fence. So now I imagine that there is another fence after the last one to take of the pressure."

I asked Daniel Deusser the same question as to the others – *Do you have a set routine at the show to prepare yourself mentally?* Daniel's response; "No, if I have a very big class, like the German championships or whatever, I try to rest a little bit before the class. Before important classes, I don't plan in any interviews. If they ask me to do something on the show I try to do it Friday or Saturday but not anymore just before the Grand Prix. Not that I have to do something special but just that I can rest a little bit, that I'm not in a hurry afterwards and that everything should be organized early enough whatever bits, bridles you want to use, so that I don't come to the stable last minute and have to change something. Normally before a Grand Prix I want to be ready in time, to just have no stress. If I ever have the feeling that I am maybe not that confident, I like to spend time on my own in the stable. When you always have people around you, they keep talking all the time, 'ah it went like this' or 'it didn't go well' all these opinions can get you down a bit. I think everybody needs to do what works well for them. Some people like to be around other people, others like to be a bit more on their own. Some riders like to listen to music or play a game on the phone to get their mind off things."

Daniel makes a good point, we are all different and so we will all respond differently to preparation routines and exercises. In fact, working with a client recently I noticed that she was so focused on the prep routine we created together that it didn't work. She had a checklist and was constantly going over it and thinking about all the things she should remember. Yes, she was doing her prep routine, but it wasn't working because she was still not trusting herself. All a prep routine needs to do is help you find that balance between being relaxed yet focused, reminding yourself of how you want to ride and at the same time letting go and trusting you will ride that way. There is no one way to create this balance, its' up to us to learn through experience and practice and then use what works well for us consistently.

To my question *Do you have a set routine at the show to prepare yourself mentally?* Edwina Tops-Alexander answered she doesn't have a set routine to get ready, yet when explaining what she does in preparation for a class, it becomes clear she does use a combination of visualization, staying positive and relaxed; "Not really as this really depends on the horse that I'm competing at the time but I try to analyze the course many times in my head and then I visualize it a few times until it's set in stone. Of course, things happen sometimes differently in the ring, so you always have to be prepared for the worst but it's definitely extremely important to stay very positive and to stay relaxed in the mind."

Olivier Philippaerts too uses visualization as a tool to get mentally ready and in flow; "When I'm in the warm up I try to visualise the course a couple of times into detail, including how I enter the arena, and how I ride in between each jump. So that by the time you get into the ring, it's automatic. So I do that a few times in my head and then when you're in the ring, it happens the way you want it to happen."

Another rider who has mastered his routine so much, he doesn't have to think about it is Michael van der Vleuten. When I asked him *Is there anything you do to mentally prepare at a show?* He answered, "No, no special things. Actually I do, I always check my whole horse before I get on to make sure the bridle and the saddle are exactly how I like it to be. For example, I hate it if it's even one hole different from how the tack is placed usually, so I always double check. Otherwise I don't have a good feeling on the horse. That should also not be a thing to worry about when you're riding."

These riders have learned through experience or from mental coaches or sport psychologists to prepare themselves as best they can. To control what they have influence over and do this routinely. They prepare mentally with visualization, physically with breathing, stretching or running depending on what they need at that moment and finally they also prepare their environment like the horse, tack and team members. Nothing is left to chance, everything is so routinely prepared for, they don't have to think about it much. Once all that is done, they can let go and trust.

Getting Into a Flow State

Of course, by now you are wondering, how can *I* get into flow? Perhaps one of the most important tasks for me as a mental coach is to help my clients be in a flow state whenever they need to perform. To become more consistent in the ring, we need to consistently prepare ourselves mentally. If we let circumstances dictate how we feel the moment we get in the saddle, our results will continue to be inconsistent.

To help my clients get into flow, I have created clear steps to easily prepare like a pro and get into a great state before getting on the horse.

First of all, as I mentioned before, if we want to be consistent in our performance, we need to prepare for it and make that preparation a habit. We don't always feel the same and the circumstances change all the time, so what we did yesterday to prepare might not work so well today. For example, imagine it's a long day at the show, you are in the last class and it's hot and humid. You have been sitting down for a few hours waiting for your class to begin. It's not a very difficult class and you don't feel particularly nervous or anxious about it. Now imagine you do a slow breathing exercise to prepare yourself... By the time you get on your horse, you will be very relaxed but not responsive or alert enough to react within a split second when needed. You will probably ride in a passive way, behind the moment not reacting quickly enough when needed. Similarly, if you are very nervous on Grand Prix day and you go for a run with heavy metal music to prepare yourself, that might not work so well either. So we want to prepare mentally according to what we need that day and at that moment, in order to get into flow.

Step 1. *Find your ideal pressure number*

In order to do that, we first need to know what our "ideal state" is. As this is very personal and at first tricky to pinpoint, I suggest we give this "ideal state" a number, so we can easily work toward it when at the show. In preparation before a show, let's assess your ideal pressure number so you can easily prepare when you are at the show. How do we do that? Consider the following statements and assess, on a scale of 1–10, to what extent it applies to you as follows: "not me at all" = **1**/10 all the way to "this is so me!" = **10**/10. For example: *"I need a lot of pressure to ride at my best"* = 6

1 **Question**
   The bigger the audience at the show, the better I ride: …
2 **Question**
   I need a lot of pressure to ride at my best: …
3 **Question**
   I don't get nervous at all thinking about competing: …
4 **Question**
   The last time I was riding really well, I was at a very important show: …
5 **Question**
   I tend to ride better during the last day(s) at a show, when the pressure is on: …
6 **Question**
   More generally, I tend to work best and most efficiently when faced with a deadline: …
7 **Question**
   I tend to ride better at the show than at home: …
8 **Question**
   I tend to ride better when my trainer puts pressure on me to do well: …
9 **Question**
   When the class is easy or small, I tend to make silly mistakes because I'm not focused enough: …
10 **Question**
   I'm not distracted at all by people watching me when I'm in the ring and I don't feel any extra pressure to do well as a result: …

Now add all your answers up and divide it by ten to get your Ideal Pressure Number (e.g. if your final score was 70, then your Ideal Pressure Number is seven on a scale of 0–10). Your ideal pressure number is the ideal level of pressure you need to perform at your best i.e. to be in flow. Know that this number might go up as you train and improve your mental game. Whenever you think your number might have changed, just take this assessment again to find out.

Step 2. *Plan for success*

Now that you are at the show, take some time to mentally prepare and get into a flow state. Find a place where you can concentrate, usually the stable, horse truck, car or restrooms work (though if you don't have the ability or time to go somewhere else, just do it wherever you are). Ideally, you plan in advance when and where you will prepare yourself mentally. Keep in mind that our end goal is to be in flow the moment we get on the horse. Your prep routine can be as long or short as you like. I usually recommend doing it within the last hour or half hour before getting on but find out what works best for you.

Step 3. *Start with two questions*

As I mentioned before, using the same exercises to prepare doesn't always guarantee flow state. The exercises you need for a given class or horse depend on how you are feeling on that day, at that moment. So, start by taking a moment to tune in. Take a few deep breaths and ask yourself, *"How am I feeling right now?"* You might feel nervous, or relaxed, tired or super excited, there is no right or wrong answer. Now that you know your "current" state, you ask yourself the second question, *"What do I need to get into my ideal number (flow) right now?"* For example, imagine that you are feeling nervous, your heart is racing and you're feeling a little tense in your upper body. It's your first time jumping a higher level and you don't know what to expect. If you would give that a number, you would be at about an eight on the pressure scale. But if your ideal number is a six, you need to do something to bring your "state" down. Similarly, you can feel great, maybe a little too relaxed, let's say a five. If your ideal number is a six, you need to use different exercises that will bring your number or state up.

Step 4. *Go through the routine you need at that moment*

Routine 1: Bring it Down

- Start with a breathing exercise to bring all of the energy that's in the upper part of your body (tense shoulders, overthinking, racing heart) down toward your lower abdomen. Start by getting into a comfortable position, with one hand on your lower abdomen (where you want to be breathing toward). Now close your eyes and take a few deep breaths in. Then, just focus on breathing in through your nose, letting it flow deep down toward your lower abdomen and breathing out through your nose again (if this is not comfortable, just breathe in and out through your mouth). An easy way to support this deep breathing is to breathe in on a count of six and out on a count of six (if six is not comfortable at first, just start with four or five and work your way up). Do know that practicing a low breathing exercise on a daily basis is very beneficial and will make it easier for you to relax when you are at a show. It is not enough to just use the breathing exercise when you need it the most, practicing this regularly will make all the difference.

- The second exercise is to visualize your best round ever and feel like you are there again. Feel the confidence in your body. Remember you have done this before and you can do it again today.
- Now, hold a very confident body posture for at least 2 minutes (think superman or wonder women). You can listen to music that helps you feel confident, relaxed and excited about riding.
- Finally, while holding your confident posture, pick one thing you will focus on when you are in the ring. We usually want too much and over-focus on riding a "perfect" or clear round. Unfortunately, our brain is not able to focus on all of the different things you need to do to be able to ride that clear round and so it get's distracted. Instead, pick one thing you want to focus on. Remember to pick something that helps you to feel, instead of think, for example, "I will keep one smooth, forward rhythm throughout the whole course."

Routine 2: Bring it Up

- Like we can bring our energy down with the breathing exercise, we can also use breathing and other exercises to bring the energy up.
- You can do all this while listening to upbeat music if you like.
- Visualize your course in great detail and if there are some difficulties around the track, visualize exactly how you will solve or avoid them.
- Like in Routine 1, pick one thing you will focus on when in the ring and direct yourself to be 100% focused, even when it is an easy class or horse.

There are, of course, more ways to help you get into your ideal number and in flow. Customize your preparation routine by adding to or exchanging some of the exercises above for whatever works for you. Ideally, you would use this preparation process every time before a class so you can make it a habit. Once it is a habit for you, you can experiment with how much time you dedicate to it. For example, even when you have very little time between classes or riding different horses, you still want to make sure you are ready and focused for the next horse. For these moments you might want to create a mini routine that works for you. Similarly, before an important class or Grand Prix, you might want to extend the routine so you can spend more time on it. You also might notice that, over time, your ideal number varies with the horse you are riding. For example, if your ideal number is a 6, but you are riding a very hot and sensitive mare, you might want to tone it down to a 5.5. I always suggest to first focus on your own ideal number until this process and way of preparing comes easily. Then, focus on the number per horse.

The best way to recognize when you are in flow is when everything seems to flow naturally, you and your horse become one and you are relaxed yet very focused. Time seems to be standing still, the distances come easily and you're having fun!

Winning Habit # 4 Flow

- The **top-down system** has the ability to analyze and reflect, focusing our attention on rational decisions instead of emotional reactions.
- When riding, **the bottom-up system** which is faster, intuitive and taps into your brain and body's experience created through thousands of hours of practice, is more helpful.
- When on the horse, **feeling** the horse underneath you will help connect with the horse, stay present and get into flow.
- **Flow is a state of consciousness** where one becomes totally absorbed in what one is doing, to the exclusion of all other thoughts and emotions. Flow is more than just focus, **flow is a harmonious experience where mind and body are working together effortlessly,** leaving the person feeling that something special has just occurred.
- Even top athletes experience **show nerves,** what matters is what we do with them. Deep breathing can help to get back into the present moment.
- **Effective riders have learned to prepare themselves as best they can.** To control what they have influence over and do this routinely. They prepare mentally with visualization, physically with breathing, stretching or running and they prepare their environment like the horse, tack and team members. Finally, they **let go and trust** that they are ready.
- In order to perform at your best, get into flow by finding your unique sweet spot between **relaxation and focus**. Take time to tune in and feel what you need at that moment. Sometimes we need to add some energy, other times we need to tone it down a bit. **Tune in, feel, trust and enjoy!**

Note

1 Source: https://www.bbc.co.uk/sport/formula1/53800895.

5 Confidence

People often believe that confidence is something you either have or you don't. It's something that may grow with positive experiences, but like talent, confidence can sometimes be (wrongly) perceived as something we are either born with, or not. Those who lack this inner confidence therefore often feel like they will never be able to do, what those with the "natural" inner conviction may be able to achieve.

Nothing could be further from the truth. In reality, confidence is built (or broken down) from the inside out by the quality of your thoughts, actions and behavior. Just like mindset, instead of perceiving confidence in terms of either having it or not, we are all on a continuous scale between low and high inner confidence, self-esteem or self-belief (in this chapter I use all these different terms to describe the same thing; confidence in ones own abilities). In order to learn how to build confidence from the inside out, we must first better understand the brain and how it may impact our confidence.

The Negativity Bias

About 80% of people who get in touch with me do so because they want to increase self-belief and work on improving their self-confidence. Some people may look confident from the outside, but are trembling on the inside. Some are confident when standing in front of a crowd or camera, but petrified in front of a horse. Others are very confident riding on home soil, but lose that self-belief when at a horseshow. Some are confident on one horse but scared on another.

Most of us know that confidence is important to do well, that is why so many clients want to work on improving it. The reason it can be challenging to stay consistently confident is that our brain is designed to keep us alive, instead of helping us to thrive. Our brain is wired to focus on anything that may be potentially dangerous to us. All the information that comes in through our senses gets checked to make sure we will stay safe. Therefore, the most primal regions of our brain – the reptilian brain and Lymbic system, don't need to focus so much on "good" or positive information, as this means we stay safe. Negative or "bad" information gets red-flagged, meaning we will most likely and instinctively focus on this type of

DOI: 10.4324/9781003204084-5

information more. The better the brain can predict what might go wrong in the future, the better it can protect us in staying alive, or so it thinks. Although this primal, subconscious reaction of the brain has helped us survive as a species and is therefore very important, it doesn't mean it's helpful when trying to increase your confidence. This explains why we generally find it a lot harder to let go of negative thoughts than positive ones. It explains why, when someone gives us a compliment we tend to spend less time thinking about that compliment than when someone gives us negative feedback. It also explains why just one mistake we made "feels" so much worse than all the great jumps combined. The primal function of the reptilian brain is to keep us alive. As a result, it doesn't like change or challenge, which is what we need to become better and to build up our confidence. It will always try to keep us where we are today with the aim to protect the identity we have created about ourselves. For example, what happens when we have created the story or identity of a 130 m rider and now you try to ride a 140 m class? Your brain will give you many reasons why it could or will go wrong. We sabotage our own progress because our primal reptilian brain doesn't like change.

In order to stay confident and able to choose the most helpful story, we need two things. First of all, we need awareness of which part of our brain is calling the shots – our rational neocortex or our emotional reptilian brain? Secondly, we need to know how to shift when the reptilian brain is controlling our thinking and with that, (most likely) our actions and results. We will discover a number of ways to increase this awareness and cultivate our most confident self later on.

How the Best Deal with Mistakes and Setbacks

One of the biggest roadblocks to a consistent and positive self-belief is the way we perceive our own mistakes and setbacks. Believing in ourselves and our chances of success is generally a lot easier when things are up than when things are down. You probably feel very different about your abilities when you have just won a class, than when you come out of the arena with 28 penalty points, for example. How can we avoid allowing the results and circumstances in our lives to dictate how we feel about ourselves, our abilities and our future?

In order to answer this question, I asked the riders I interviewed about how they perceive failure, deal with mistakes and setbacks. Not surprisingly, their answers were very much in line with the research from author and journalist, Matthew Syed, which we will learn more about later.

Laura Kraut reminds us of the fact that we are all human including our idols and everyone, idols included, can make mistakes. In Laura's words; "Everyone makes mistakes in this sport and everyone, even at the highest level can do diabolical things. I am no exception, there will be times that I go into the ring and make mistakes."

It's the way these riders deal with their mistakes, however, which makes the difference. Laura chooses a relaxed acceptance and moves on, put simply; "I just shrug it off. Obviously you are upset, but like the other night I had a mistake in the jump off, the mare didn't understand me and basically tore out the entire jump and a lot of people made fun of me when I got out the ring, but it doesn't bother me one bit! We all make mistakes. I have seen Ludger [Beerbaum] do it, I have seen Nick [Skelton] do it, and I have seen Simon Delestre and Scott Brash do it. I have done it right a thousand times before and I will probably do it another thousand times."

Lorenzo De Luca teaches us another valuable lesson, that it's ok to be upset but there has to be a limit on how long emotions are allowed to take over. Lorenzo explains; "For sure it's not nice for us, the horses, the team or the people watching, but in the end everyone makes mistakes. You are angry with yourself the first hour – which is good. It helps you to think about your mistake. But then it is also important to let it go and not overthink your mistakes, to focus also on the positive. Because if we were all perfect, in this sport, it would be boring."

After having some initial time to be upset, than having evaluated on how to learn from what happened, it's important to take the next step and look forward and find out how to train your "weakness" so it can become your strength. Laura Klaphake explains it in her own words; "Sometimes you have to look back to see what you did wrong. But once you analyze this, you have to look forward. It makes no sense to look backwards anymore. You don't get better if you just look backwards."

Instead of mistakes being something we need a few days to get over and it being a distraction to our progress, it can also be seen as feedback and therefore guidance to improvement. In fact, as we learned in Chapter 1, when in a growth mindset, negative feedback can even be perceived as something positive, as it's a sign of being in the growth zone. Edwina Tops-Alexander said; "Of course I get frustrated when I make mistakes but sometimes it's a reminder for me and it keeps me on my toes. Setbacks actually get me more motivated to improve."

In the case of Piergiorgio Bucci, dealing with mistakes and failure in a positive way was not one of his strengths, he could be very hard on himself. That said, as we have learned so far, everything is trainable including our mental resilience. When I asked him how he deals with failure, PG said; "Now, very good, because of the books I've read and mental coaching. Before, I was terrible. I would be very mean to myself, even if it wasn't my fault. Now I know, mistakes happen, so I am prepared and I just want to learn from it so it happens less often or not again. Also, I have learned to laugh at myself more and not take myself too serious."

Finally, Cian O'Connor touches on a very important point and that is to keep thinking with the long-term plan in mind. Instead of thinking only of this mistake at this show or the next or this year's championship, Cian teaches us to focus on consistency in the long run. Will you still be thinking about the mistake you made today 10 years from now? If the answer is no, then learn from it what you can and move on quickly. In Cian's words; "I try to keep a positive from everything. I have had ups and downs in my life, both in personal and in sport. I suppose you learn from every situation. It's not a race, it's about longevity. You keep working. I came back and I won my bronze medal in London and I won a gold and bronze in 2017 in Gothenburg. To keep putting yourself out there as a major player in the sport you get respect and time moves on. It's a business and I am hugely more successful than I was 5 years ago or 5 years before that."

As Cian demonstrates, though mistakes and setbacks can greatly trigger the negativity-bias and decrease confidence, when deliberately and consistently working toward the long-term goal, you allow yourself to learn, adjust, move on and ultimately succeed.

Challenges and Self-Doubt

Whether through education, upbringing or self-teaching, those who are successful in sport and business have learned to deal with challenges and failure in an effective way. They love to win, but they also know how to lose. That doesn't mean however that they have never struggled or experienced self-doubt. The following examples from Jeroen Dubbeldam and Olivier Philippaerts show that even the best have had times where they felt like giving up. Their advice? Stay patient and keep going. Bad moments will pass and when you persevere, you get out even stronger than when you started.

Talking to Jeroen Dubbeldam, he explained how he didn't always work the way he works now. There was a time where he would ride horses only for a short period of time, riding to win classes, rather than improving the horses so they could be sold quickly. Then, when he moved back to The Netherlands a fellow equestrian introduced him to a new way of thinking. A long-term, improvement-focused way of training. Jeroen decided to give this growth-focused and deliberate training system a go, but it wasn't as easy as he anticipated.

In Jeroen's own words; "In the beginning I was working for dealing stables all the time. First with my father of course and then in Switzerland for Gerhard Etter. At that time we only focused on short term, quick turnover. Get on a horse and get the quickest result possible, which is the opposite of how I work now. At that time, we always had different horses, you had a horse for one, two or three shows maximum and then they were gone. It was a quick sort of thing, which is a totally different approach to when I came to Holland and I got some owners that supported me and I got to keep horses for a longer time. That's when you have to approach the whole thing in a totally different way and you need to go with the horse for a long-term career."

When asked about this transition Jeroen admits, "Yes it was difficult, a difficult step. I came to Holland and I wasn't working for Hans [Horn], but we had our horses based there. We tried to shift into that programme and it was very hard in the beginning because I had to focus on things I never even thought about before. I was used to riding on pure, natural instinct and now I had to work a horse, improve the body of a horse, make it stronger, make it loose, make his mind, become a team together. I found it very hard in the beginning because you face a lot of problems when you start doing that."

"Like when you try to find control over a horse in the course you face a lot of problems. For example, you feel that the horse is not strong enough or maybe it jumps a little to the right there and then you start working on those things to make it better. In that process it first gets a little bit worse before it can get better. It's hard because at first you were just going to shows and you didn't think about that. You win classes and you go home and you go to the next show. But now I didn't win classes, because I was improving my horses and I was there to try to improve things. So then you go home and instead of having won three classes you had one or two down."[1]

Jeroen touches on a key point here. An important element to any kind of transformation or change is that the first part always starts with, what I like to call, chaos. *"In that process it first gets a little bit worse before it can get better."* Coming out of our comfort zone, having to stretch ourselves is never easy nor comfortable and can really decrease our confidence. I asked Jeroen how this transition impacted his confidence, did he doubt whether he was good enough?

"At that point, yes. When I started to do that and it didn't really work from the beginning, I thought 'oh my God' I made the wrong decision to do this, because I'm not good enough and this and that. Before you go to the shows and you win classes and you go home and you didn't even think about those things. And now you start doubting yourself."

"It took me a while but then, once you come through that process and it starts to work then after a while, you get an even bigger result than you ever did before. That gives you confidence that you can do it. Then from then on, I approached every horse like that."

This "transformation" period ended up taking two long years and when I asked Jeroen how he managed to get through it he said, "I don't know, it was a process, I was close to giving up. To either go back to be the rider I was before or maybe go and find something else."

Luckily Jeroen didn't give up and stuck to it, trusting himself and the new system of continuously improving his horses. Even though it did impact his confidence initially, growing into his growth mindset and feeling his horses develop, ultimately helped him not only become a stronger rider and winning many championships including the Olympic title, his confidence grew stronger than before because he learned how to lose in order to become better.

Olivier Philippaerts also openly talked about self-doubt with me and admitted he has had many moments when he doubted himself; "When you have a bad moment and it doesn't go like you wanted it to go, you get in a bad place. Yes of course, people have those moments and thoughts and maybe in the future these doubts come back. Because it's always ups and downs but I think also the ups and downs, they become more normal and you know they can come, but they can leave also."

Asking how Olivier deals with these challenging moments he replied; "I think I know that they will leave so I just keep on going. I just know things will change again, so don't always keep thinking "oh, what if they [horses] go bad." No, I just keep going. If you stick to your system, it will change. For example, imagine your horse has one [bar] down [which means having four penalty points], three shows or classes in a row, but it jumps really well, then stay patient and the results will come back."

It's easy to feel good about our abilities when doing well but being resilient means, you believe in yourself no matter what. That doesn't mean you don't ever feel scared or experience nerves, it just means you do what you need to do in order to ride your best performance possible.

When we allow ourselves to go through these ups and downs, we realize that failure, mistakes and challenges are all part of growth. In fact, it is the struggle that makes us stronger, without it success would not be the same. As Mark Twain put it, "What is success without failure? What is a win, without a loss?"

Redefining Failure

What is your first thought or reaction when you read the word failure? Most of us think of failure as something negative, something to avoid at all cost. In fact, some of us might even ride into the competition arena with one goal in mind: don't make any mistakes. Some of you exit the arena and the first thing you do is criticize yourself for the one mistake you made, not noticing the twelve other jumps that were great. Failure is a loaded word for most of us; however, when I asked the riders I interviewed about how they deal with failure, making mistakes and coping with setbacks, I was stunned by the re-semblance of all their answers and their view on failure. What I have learned as a result, is that the way we view failure has a huge impact on our confidence and our ability to keep learning and growing in the sport.

Dealing with failure better requires us to change the way we view failure in the first place. In his book *Black Box Thinking*, Matthew Syed, author, journalist and former Olympian himself shows us how to do just that. He reveals how different people, businesses and industries deal with failure and why they have become successful, or not. According to Syed, "Black Box Thinking is about the willingness and tenacity to investigate the lessons that often exist when we fail, but which we rarely exploit."[2] In essence, Syed suggests we not merely deal with making mistakes but rather, use our mistakes to improve. He said, "The explanation for success hinges, in powerful and often counter-intuitive ways, on how we react to failure." Working with many clients over the years, I can attest that often the biggest block holding these athletes back is their fear of failure.

Perhaps one of the biggest triggers for this fear is the fixed mindset. As we learned in Chapter 1, a fixed mindset creates this idea that failure is a direct result of a lack of talent and abilities; therefore, making mistakes is something we must avoid at all cost. Paradoxically, this mindset creates a pattern of making the same mistakes over and over again because we fail to learn from them. We are so afraid to fail we don't dare to try anything new or really look at what we need to improve and so we stay in our comfort zone, repeating what doesn't work.

In *Black Box Thinking*, Syed shares a powerful study to underline why redefining failure is crucial to continues learning, consistent confidence and success. "Consider an experiment involving a group of schoolchildren who had shown difficulty in dealing with failure. In that respect, they were like many of us. Half of these students were then given a course where they experienced consistent success. The questions posed during these sessions were easy and the students were delighted to ace them. They began to develop intellectual self-confidence, as you would expect.

The second group were not given successes, but training in how to reinterpret their failures. They were sometimes given problems they couldn't solve, but were also taught to think they could improve if they expended effort. The failures were positioned not as indications of their lack of intelligence, but as opportunities to improve their reasoning and understanding. At the end of these training courses, the two groups were tested on a difficult problem. Those who had experienced consistent success were as demoralized by failing to solve this problem as they had been before the training. They were so sensitive to failure that their performance declined and it took many days for them to recover. Some were even more afraid of challenges and didn't want to take risks. The group that had been taught to reinterpret failure were quite different. They significantly improved in their ability to deal with the challenging task. Many actually demonstrated superior performance after failure and when they went back to class began asking their teachers for more challenging work. Far from ducking out of situations where they might fail, they embraced them."

What this study shows is that consistent confidence doesn't grow from positive results alone. Yes, confidence often increases when getting a good result, but the moment we fail, our confidence drops down again, sometimes even further down than it used to be in the first place. Instead, this study clearly shows the importance of learning to interpret failure differently. To see failure not as proof that we are no good, but as feedback to how we can get better.

Redefining failure and with that, responding differently to it, is particularly important in equestrian sport as the horse, which is incredibly intuitive and has a need of confidence of its own, picks up and often responds to peoples confidence or a lack thereof. The moment a rider's confidence drops and self-doubt kicks in, the horse will pick up on the subtle differences in how the rider communicates with his or her aids. This in turn can lead to a horse losing confidence in the rider or taking advantage of the situation and so refusing to jump further. It is therefore the important task of a rider to learn how to deal with making mistakes or a lack of confidence in the ring. That said, this is not an easy task to master from 1 day to another, don't be too hard on yourself in the process, stay patient and remember to focus on improvement over perfection.

Let's discover how exactly we can redefine failure to learn from its valuable lessons and increase confidence. Here follows an exercise to help you do that.

Step number one is to start by putting in words and on paper, how you have been viewing failure until today. You can do this by finishing the following sentence; "Failing to me means I ...."

Take a moment to evaluate how helpful your statement or belief really is. Once you know whether your way of viewing your mistakes has been helping you or holding you back, you can redefine failure in a helpful way (if necessary).

Step number two is to write down, in a few sentences how you will perceive failure from now on. Here is an example, which you can repeat to yourself, and most importantly, live by every day.

The mistakes I make are feedback on my training, my preparation and my mental game. They say little about me and everything about my performance in this moment. If my performance was not what I wanted it to be, I was either not prepared enough, not focused and present enough, not trusting (myself and/or horse) enough, or I haven't trained in the appropriate way. Using the three-step reflection (from Chapter 1), I will now use this feedback to deliberately work on improving my brain and body to perform differently next time.

Step number 3: remember the three-step reflection exercise we have learned in Chapter 1? Commit to using it every evening to reflect on your day, training and/or competition to help you (re) focus on improvement and learning from your mistakes.

Three-step reflection questions:

1   What went well?
2   What could have been better?
3   How will I improve this? (Make a plan and plan it in)

Winning Habit Number 5: Consistent Confidence

As we have learned so far in this Chapter, true confidence doesn't depend on circumstances or rise and fall with your results. Self-belief and unwavering inner confidence are consciously built from the inside out and can cherish the good times and withstand the bad times. How do we do that? By taking an inner stance and aligning our thoughts, spoken words, beliefs, body language and actions, with the most confident version of ourselves. We all have had moments already in our lives where we acted and felt confident. Go back to a moment when you felt really confident. It can be a small moment, or a big one. It's about how you felt, thought and acted that moment in time, not how the situation unfolded necessarily (if no memory comes to mind, continue to ask yourself this question over the next 2 days). Where were you? What was the weather like? How did you show up that day? How did you walk, talk and behave that day? If how you showed up that day is different from how you show up on a daily basis, it's very likely you will not be feeling consistently confident. In order to feel deeply confident we must consistently talk, think and act in accordance with this confidence inside us. Applying the following traits will help you do that.

Deliberate Action

As we have learned at the beginning of this chapter, our brain can sabotage our confidence and provide us with many good reasons why we can't do something and why, the moment it get's physically or mentally uncomfortable, we should give up. This negativity bias didn't stop Michael Jordan though, during the 1997 NBA finals. The Bulls were tied 2–2 and heading into the final and decisive game. Michael Jordan needs to play his A-game if they want to have a chance of bringing home the NBA championship title. There is one problem however, Michael has come down with a bad food poisoning overnight. For most people that would be it, we would listen to our reptilian brain that is telling us to stay in bed and don't play, let alone to go out and win. Michael went out and played for 44 minutes, scoring 38 points and with that greatly contributing to winning their 5th championship title.

We can do whatever we set our mind to. Michael was able to score those 38 points because he had trained his mind and body for years leading up to that moment. He had created a strong commitment to doing whatever it takes, so much so that not even actual, significant illness could stop him. The moral of this story is, that confidence is built through committing 100% to your goals and process. Smart, deliberate action leads to growth and competence, which leads to confidence, which leads to great results. Next time you don't feel confident, go take deliberate action anyway and don't stop until you reach your goal.

A way of training our brain to commit fully to our goals instead of endlessly going over our mistakes is by using visualization. How often do you go over the mistakes you made on the weekend or in your last training session? How often do you remind yourself of the mistakes and the feelings of disappointment that come with it? Many of us think about this regularly if not consistently and as a result emphasize the neural network in our brain that says, "I messed up again," "I'm not good enough." This is a recipe for low self-esteem. So we need to train our brain to think better in order to do better. As described in Chapter 2, regularly visualizing a great ride or competition helps to remind your brain of how you want to ride and that you have already done well in the past. You can go over this memory in its entirety or add moments of great rides together to create your very own highlight real. For example, you can have parts of the first round and then parts of a jump off and lastly, a moment in a prize giving ceremony. What matters here is that these memories make you feel proud and confident. You want to not only remember that moment, but more importantly, feel as if you're riding like that again, breathing the same way, holding the same body posture, feeling that same confident feeling knowing you are in control. Start small with a few minutes of reminding yourself of these memories and expand over time with how you would like to ride in the future.

Language

I use the word language in this context to describe the spoken words we use in conversation with others, as well as our inner dialogue, the conscious and subconscious thoughts we have. Many of these thoughts and even the words we speak out loud, are not carefully chosen but rather habitual. Like all the other habits in our life, we need to become aware of which ones are helpful and which ones are not.

For example, imagine one of your friends would spend a whole day by your side. Imagine that your friend uses negative language consistently. The whole day you hear him say, "you are not good enough," "why bother, it's not going to work anyway" and "you might as well give up, you will never make it." How would you feel at the end of the day? Most of us would feel drained, down and defeated. Hopefully you will never allow anyone to treat you like that. The question is, however, do you ever treat yourself like that? All too often these are thoughts that run through our own mind, day after day. All too often, we allow our own (reptilian) brain to bring us down. It is estimated that we have between 50.000 and 70.000 thoughts a day! It is also estimated that 70% of those thoughts are the same, day in and day out. Could it be that after a few setbacks combined with our negativity bias, this 70% becomes mostly negative? This unhelpful self-talk is bound to have a profound impact on our confidence. This is why it's so important that we become aware of the thoughts, language and body language we use on a daily basis and know how to change it when necessary.

Let me give you another example of the impact of negative self-talk. The other day I was in a spin class and at first, it felt great. I felt fit and while the instructor kept telling us to increase and add a gear, I was able to keep up. Until, about 10 minutes into the class. Suddenly my body gave up and I could not keep up my RPM. Already after a few minutes my mind started to follow and gave up too. Thoughts arrived like, "I am not as fit as I thought I was," "I haven't been training enough," "why am I always the worst of the class" and so on. Suddenly I noticed that my RPM moved up or down together with the quality of my thoughts. As I got direct feedback from my bike, I couldn't help but notice that with those negative thoughts, my body gave up even more. This is what used to happen on the horse as well. With every tiny mistake I made, I would beat myself up and therefore be even more distracted. On top of that, my horses would often react to that and we would be off on a negative downward spiral.

Similarly, when we talk to our friends, trainers, spouses or parents, what kind of language do we use? The other day, a client told me that while in conversation with her mom, talking about riding a young horse, her mom caught her saying "I'm such a wimp" three times within a few minutes. She hadn't noticed it herself so she was surprised when her mom pointed it out. What are the words and phrases you use regularly to describe yourself? If we are not careful, these words, this language we use repeatedly, can become a "story." A story we start to believe about who we are as a rider.

Getting annoyed and self-critical after making mistakes and using language that brings you down is not a solution to the problem. Usually, it only adds to the problem. Many believe that being very hard and critical will help to do better next time, but ask yourself; "have I improved my riding, confidence or any other skills as a result of being so hard on myself?" I guarantee you, the answer is no.

If being critical and beating yourself up is not helpful, then what you may wonder? Asking quality questions! What went well? What could have been better? How will I improve this? How will I make it happen? Who do I need to be to get the job done? What do I need to do differently next time? How will I practice that at home? What else? What else? Write these helpful questions down and use, read and repeat them regularly for yourself.

Apart from regularly asking quality questions, here is a way to become aware and let go of unhelpful language. The words and thoughts we use are often an automatic response, a habit, which is something we can change. A fun way to do this is to ask some of your friends or family members to play a game with you. Every time anyone mentions a negative word or uses language that brings down your, their own, or anyone else's confidence, that person (who could be you!)

should be made aware of it, and the word or language noted. The person who uses the least "unhelpful" words that day, week or month will receive a fun reward. Once you are more aware of the patterns and triggers of what language you use and when you use it the most, you can now make a plan to replace those words with more fun, positive, uplifting and helpful ones. Start with one word you use often that you would like to replace and think of what word(s) you could best replace them with. Continue for as long as you notice you still use words or thoughts that trigger insecurity. In the meantime, keep it fun and remember there is no need or point to beat yourself up. Changing habits takes time and repetition but it will be well worth the effort.

Changing the Narrative

As mentioned above, the habitual words we use to describe ourselves often create a story in our head about who we believe to be and what we believe we are able of achieving. What is the story you tell yourself and others about yourself as a rider? For example, when somebody who has no clue about the equestrian sport asks you, "so, are you any good?" What do you reply? Are you aware of how your "story" is either supporting you and your self-confidence or how it might bring you down? Most often, it doesn't matter how much others believe in us, the whole world can tell us we are incredibly powerful, beautiful, successful, if we don't believe it ourselves, it won't make any difference to our confidence. If our story, our internal narrative, is not supporting and helping us, we are not able to reach our full potential and we are rarely the best version of ourselves. When this happens, we are constantly listening to our fears, instead of our true potential. I don't need to tell you how that story ends.

Let's look at an exercise I often use with my clients. Get pen and paper, and answer the question above – what is the story you tell yourself and others about who you are and your abilities as a rider? Allow yourself time for this exercise. You don't have to answer it all in one go. Notice what you tell your trainer, friends or family when reflecting on your training or competition. Think about your perceived limits of what you are able to do.

Once you have written down your "old story." Take a moment to get comfortable, take a few deep breaths and read this story to yourself. What do you notice in your body while, or after reading this? Does this story lift you up or bring you down? If it's the latter, no need to panic, take another deep breath and remember the good news, you can change your narrative at any time. When you are ready for that next step, ask three people that know you (and your riding) well, like your trainer, friends and/or family members, to write down for you what they believe your strengths are. Now, together with this feedback, write down a new story for yourself. Make sure that when you read it, you feel excited and more confident. Now reread (and add to) your story every day for the next 3 weeks (or longer if you like).

Body Language

Apart from our thoughts and the spoken language we use, there is another type of language that has a powerful impact on our confidence. Let's turn to the work of Amy Cuddy, a social psychologist, expert on the behavioral science of power, presence and prejudice and best-selling author of the book *Presence*. Cuddy suggests that the way we hold our bodies can have a powerful impact on the way we think. In her famous Ted Talk, "Your Body Language May Shape Who You Are" she explains how we can affect our own thoughts, feelings and performance and become more present, influential, brave and satisfied.[3] Cuddy shares how in one of her studies, participants were asked to hold an insecure body posture (think shoulders hunched, chin to chest, small posture). After only a few minutes of holding this insecure body posture, cortisol (a stress hormone) increased in the participant's blood and testosterone (a dominance or confidence hormone) dropped. On the other hand, holding a very confident body posture (think – superman/wonder women pose) resulted in the opposite. Cortisol dropped and testosterone increased, leaving the participants feeling more confident and powerful after only a few minutes of holding the pose. Although her findings received criticism from fellow psychologists, I decided to test them for myself.

I began walking around and holding a very confident body posture when I needed a confidence boost, like when presenting a workshop or standing in front of a group. I noticed it indeed contributed to me feeling more confident and in charge. I thought about the riders I worked with and how they could benefit, so I suggested they try it too. When walking the course, I suggested walking using their most confident body language, just like ultra-confident athletes such as Usain Bolt and Kent Farrington. When feeling insecure on the horse, I suggest doing the same and "fake it till you make it." Or, like Cuddy puts it, "Fake it till you feel it."

Your first reaction might be, "but that's not me," or "I don't want to be arrogant." I get it. Many of my clients have a similar reaction. However, there is a big difference between arrogance and confidence. The first is feeling like you are better than others. The second, confidence, is feeling like the best version of yourself. You can be confident and humble at the same time. I sent some clients out to find their inner confidence by holding a power (think superhero) pose[4] or walking chest out and chin up. As a result of my experiment, my clients came back to tell me that walking around with a confident body posture made a big difference for them, much more than they expected.

Own Who You Really Are

So far we have learned to redefine failure in a way that helps us to learn from our mistakes rather than fight them. We have learned to use more positive and helpful language instead of criticizing ourselves. All this helps us to become more aware of our strengths and to realize it's much more helpful to own this part of ourselves than to downplay it. What I have learned in working with many riders that are, just like myself, very hardworking perfectionists who set the bar very high for themselves, is that we not only have to accept our strengths and own them, we also need to embrace and fully accept our weaknesses. That is often a lot harder to do as we shy away from it. We don't like to see that part of ourselves that has made the same mistake again or that has failed or fallen down again. What happens if we don't face this part of ourselves? We continue to make the same mistakes over and over again. We don't progress because we can't accept the consequences of making mistakes or failing and so we are still holding on to it. This might sound strange at first, how do you hold on to it if you really don't want something to happen? Think about a mistake you made once that felt really bad at the time (or still). What was it that made it so bad? Did you feel angry, embarrassed or deeply disappointed? Whatever it is, you did not, or maybe still don't, accept reality. Reality is we are human and we all mess up! As long as you fight it, you give it power. If you can't accept that you make mistakes or do something stupid sometimes, you are attached to a certain outcome. All this means you are not accepting every part of yourself. Real freedom and real inner confidence come when we can really accept every part of ourselves – the good, the bad and the ugly.

As Daniel Deusser said, "Every failure is a lesson, if you are not willing to fail, you are not ready to succeed." In order to fully accept every part of yourself, you need to learn to forgive yourself. This may seem a little heavy but if you can't forgive yourself for whatever it is you have done, your confidence will continue to fluctuate and depend on your performance and outcome. Daniel also talked about staying authentic instead of trying to imitate someone else, "Don't ever try to imitate somebody. I saw so many people who sit on the horse like somebody else or try to do things because somebody else does it. I think you need to have your own style, need to think about your own style. You can think about the way other riders think and train, you can always learn a little more but never try to imitate them."

Owning who you really are starts with accepting yourself as you are, forgiving yourself for messing up and at the same time realizing that you are already great just the way you are. Only then will you realize that you are already good enough today. In the Disney film Mulan, a young girl is taught to become someone she is not. She has an incredible power inside her but even though her parents love her very much, they convince her to hide that part of herself away and to be just like every other girl in town. Mulan does as she is told because she doesn't want to bring shame to her family. One day, in order to protect her father, she takes his place to fight in a war to protect the emperor. As she is challenged continuously in many different ways, she realizes her and her regiment won't survive unless she steps into who she really is. Luckily, as you would expect in a Disney film, Mulan lets go of the fear of failure and humiliation in order to save the emperor and the empire. She stops playing small in order to fit in and instead reveals her true self and steps into her true power.

Though it's a Disney film, to me Mulan is a great metaphor that highlights the importance of daring to step into our true potential. Daring to step into our true power and own who we really are. Have you ever pulled something off that you didn't think you could? Did you ever ride into a class thinking, "I don't stand a chance" only to ride a clear round? You are already good enough just the way you are today. Now it's time you start to really step into that and believe it too.

A great example of someone who has learned to step into her own authentic power, regardless of all the opinions about her appearance, is show jumping rider Danielle Goldstein Waldman. Dani stands out from the usual horseshow crowd, she dresses differently and wears bright feathers in her hair. Many conservative equestrians seem to have an opinion about her unique appearance, but Dani explains in her social media feed; "No one should feel bad about the choices they make that make them feel good about themselves. I wear my feathers because I feel great about them. It's good to be different. Embrace individuality. Embrace that difference. There is no need to look the same. Promote kindness and individuality and feel good about yourself. That will reflect in your results in the sport and everything else you do in life." Dani has since created the #ownyouRIDEntity movement, encouraging others to feel empowered, beautiful and to #ownit! Expressing her unique individuality and with that stepping into her power has helped Dani become more confident not only as a person but as a rider in the saddle as well.

Comparing Ourselves

Generally, when comparing yourself to other riders it is tempting to fall into the trap of comparing yourself to riders who you believe are better than you or have better circumstances, horses or resources. We tend to notice all of their great rounds, and then compare that to our bad rounds and mistakes. Even though we know it's not helpful and it often brings us down, comparing ourselves to others, whether in real life or on social media is a recipe for a meltdown. When talking to Daniel Deusser he confessed he was not always as confident as he is today and he too used to compare himself to his "idols" which brought his confidence down.

"In the beginning, I was always thinking that the other people were better than me. But I don't think about that anymore. The ones who train better and who are more experienced can be better or make better decisions in the ring than the others. But basically we are all human beings working together with animals and we have to try to work together, train together, get the feeling together. But nobody is better than the other one."

From now on, whenever you compare yourself or look up to other riders, just compare yourself to where you were yesterday. Have you improved? If so, great! If not, do what you need to do to improve today. It can be helpful to learn from other riders and what they do well, but it's equally important to look at what you already do well and continue to work, one step at a time, to improve.

Creating Consistent Confidence

Building consistent confidence from the inside out is a process and it requires continuous awareness. The exercises in this chapter all contribute to enhancing different elements of your inner self-belief. Using them regularly will not only help to become more aware of your own behavior but also show you how to change it where needed. Here is a quick reminder of all the practical exercises mentioned in this chapter. Use, implement and utilize these regularly to get consistent results.

Exercise 1. Redefining failure

Step 1.
Become aware of how you have perceived failure up to this point by asking yourself (and writing down) *"Failing to me means I ..."*

Step 2.
Now write down how you want to view failure instead.

Step 3.
Reflect on each day using the three-step reflection mentioned in Chapter 1.

Exercise 2. Visualizing your best round ever

Whether you need some extra confidence before an important competition or you are working on your inner belief in general, visualizing your best performance ever is a helpful way to remind your brain of exactly how you want to ride in the future.

Exercise 3. Changing the narrative

Step 1.
Get pen and paper, and answer the question: what is the story you tell yourself and others about who you are and your abilities as a rider? It may help to notice what you tell your trainer, friends or family when reflecting on your training or competition. Also, think about your perceived limits of what you are capable of.

Step 2.

Take a moment to get comfortable, take a few deep breaths and read this story to yourself. What do you notice in your body while, or after reading this? Does this story lift you up or bring you down? If it's the latter, no need to panic, take another deep breath and remember the good news, you can change your narrative at any time. If you want, you can tear up this story and throw it away.

Step 3.

Now ask three people that know you (and your riding) well (trainer, best friends or family members), to write down for you what they believe your strengths are. Now, together with this feedback, write down a new story for yourself. Make it as positive as you can.

Step 4.

Make sure that when you read it, you feel excited and uplifted. Now reread (and continue to add to) your story every day for the next 3 weeks (or as long as you like).

Exercise 4. Ask quality questions

Write down quality questions that help you forward and repeat them regularly for yourself. Examples are:

What went well? What could have been better? How will I improve this? What would I have done differently if I couldn't feel fear? How will I make it happen next time? Who do I need to be, to get the job done? What do I need to do differently next time? How will I practice that at home? What else? What else?

Exercise 5. Language awareness game

Step 1.

Invite your friends and/or family to play this "negative language game" with you.

Step 2.

Determine a time frame and end reward. Within this day, week or month, every time anyone mentions a negative word or uses language that brings down your, their own, or anyone else's confidence get four penalty points.

Step 3.

The person who uses the least "unhelpful" words that day, week or month and thus has the least penalty points, will receive a fun reward.

Step 4.

Once you are more aware of the negative words you often use and when you use it the most, you can now make a plan to replace those words with more fun, positive, uplifting and helpful language. Start with one word you use often that you would like to replace and think of what word(s) you could best replace them with.

Step 5.

Continue for as long as you notice you still use words or thoughts that trigger insecurity.

Exercise 6. Power posing

In preparation for an important meeting, event, presentation or competition, hold a power pose (Google "Superman/Wonder women power pose" if needed) for a few minutes and bring out the most confident version of you as you walk into the arena.

Exercise 7. Own who you are

In order to own who you truly are you need two things. Number one is qto accept every part of yourself and to forgive yourself for mistakes you made in the past. And secondly, you need to step into your authentic power.

Step 1. Take a post–it note or small paper and write down, "I forgive myself for …"

Hang this on your bathroom mirror. Now commit for the next 7 days to start your morning by finishing that sentence. There might be one thing that will come up every morning, in that case, forgive yourself for that same thing every single morning until you feel it's no longer holding power over you. If every morning it's something else or something small, that's great too.

Step 2. Take that same (post it) note and write underneath the first sentence, "I am proud of myself for …" Aim to add not only achievements here but also anything that makes you unique and strong. Commit for the next 7 days to answer this question for yourself.

You can do steps 1 and 2 at the same time or start with one and after 7 days, do the other. If you feel it's helpful for you after these 7–14 days, by all means do continue to use it.

Winning habit # 5 Confidence

- **Our brain is wired to focus on anything** that may be potentially **dangerous or negative** to us. In order to stay confident, we need awareness of which part of our brain is calling the shots – our rational neocortex, or our emotional reptilian brain. Secondly, we need to know how to shift when the reptilian brain is controlling our thinking, actions and results.
- It's easy to feel good about our abilities when doing well but **being resilient means, you believe in yourself no matter what.** That doesn't mean you don't ever feel scared or experience nerves, it just means you do what you need to do in order to ride your best performance possible.
- Though mistakes and setbacks can greatly trigger the negativity bias and decrease confidence, when deliberately and consistently working toward the **long-term goal**, you allow yourself to **learn, adjust, move on and ultimately succeed.**
- Consistent confidence doesn't grow from positive results alone. Yes, confidence often increases when getting a good result, but the moment we fail, our confidence drops down again, sometimes even further down than it used to be in the first place. It's important therefore that we learn to **interpret failure differently. To see failure not as proof that we are no good, but as feedback to how we can get better.**
- Other ways to create consistent confidence from the inside out are; **Taking deliberate and consistent action toward your goals,** using **helpful (body) language, focus on a helpful perspective** and **step into your authentic power.**

Notes

1 Jeroen describes here important elements of teaching a horse to jump a certain way and to correctly respond to the riders' aids. Doing this greatly increases the chances of jumping without making mistakes. In order to get the desired results on important championships however, the horse needs to be trained at home, as well as in the show ring, to create correct and consistent communication between horse and rider.
2 https://www.samuelthomasdavies.com/book-summaries/business/black-box-thinking/.
3 https://www.amycuddy.com.
4 A power pose is basically standing feet firmly planted hip width apart, chest out, chin up and hands on the hips.

6   Motivation

Just like our mindset and confidence, the level of motivation we experience in any given moment fluctuates on a spectrum between low and high. It is rarely in one place forever. Meaning, there are days where we feel very motivated to take action, to be the best version of ourselves to train deliberately and improve. But there are also days when we don't feel like doing anything. Most often, motivation goes up when things go well but when results or certain outcomes are not there (yet), motivation drops. Just like confidence, motivation often rises and falls with our level of performance. I see this a lot in working with my clients, it's not easy to stay focused and patient when the results are not there to show for it.

Although the concept of motivation has similarities to the other concepts in this book, it also has some differences. Unlike the other concepts explained in the previous chapters, motivation comes forth from an accumulation of different factors. The topics discussed so far in this book from mindset to deliberate training, flow and confidence, all impact our motivation in a significant way. Therefore, having learned about and hopefully started to implement the different tools and exercises learned in this book so far, will all contribute to a deeper level of motivation. Now let's unpack motivation further and learn how we can motivate ourselves in a balanced and sustainable way and turn motivation into commitment and commitment into action.

Start with Why

In order to learn how to create consistent motivation to train and be at our best, paradoxically we need to start by looking backward first. According to Simon Sinek, bestselling author of multiple books on leadership and business including *Start With Why*,[1] we must inspire ourselves and others in order to succeed in the long run, not manipulate. In other words, instead of dragging ourselves out of bed in the morning claiming it will be a good day, we must inspire ourselves to be at our best and make it a good day, regardless of the results or circumstances. A very powerful question that can help fuel this intrinsic inspiration and with that, motivations is "why do I do what I do?." This applies to sport just as much as it does to business.

DOI: 10.4324/9781003204084-6

So why do you do what you do? Let's take a moment to go back in time. Do you remember your first interaction with a horse? What about your first ride? I bet you were not thinking about results or doing well, you were just excited to connect with such a magical animal, the idea that you could look after and work together with this amazing being. The partnership and friendship was the most special thing about it. This was the case for me when I started anyway. Until the day I won my first competition. I can still remember the excitement, the thrill, the addictive feeling of success. Once I tasted this, I wanted more. Slowly I forgot about why I started and focused more and more on winning and that amazing feeling that comes with it. It is easy to imagine how for many of us, the thrill of winning can cloud our minds and distract us from the most important aspect of our journey, our "why" which often is the simple but profound love for horses.

Why is this important? Because your unique "why" gives direction to your life. When I'm reminded of the love for horses I think of the exciting power of becoming a team together with a horse. Learning from them as much as teaching them. Growing together to become one when the pressure is on. When this is my why, I will be very focused on this connection. When I lose track of my why and crave the result and the need to prove that I am better than someone else, I lose motivation the moment I don't get those results. Sinek describes it as follows in his book *Start With Why*: "All organizations start with WHY, but only the great ones keep their WHY clear year after year. Those who forget WHY they were founded show up to the race every day to outdo someone else instead of to outdo themselves. The pursuit, for those who lose sight of WHY they are running the race, is for the medal or to beat someone else."

I often ask my clients the following question when they are feeling really nervous or scared, "why are you at this competition?" Are you here to be perfect? Are you here to beat everyone else? Are you here to not fail? OR, are you here to be the best version of yourself, to connect, learn and grow with your horse and to enjoy the ride? Of course, the latter answer is, for most of us, why we do what we do, but we lose track of this too often.

Interviewing the riders for this book, I was inspired by how much they were in touch with their why. Their motivation to consistently train hard comes forth from a deep love and passion for their horses and feeling them improving.

Love for Horses

The drive for these riders to keep going even when the going gets tough comes forth from a deep love for improvement and the sport itself, but above all, the love for horses. At the heart of why these riders do what they do, almost every single day of the year, is a deep-rooted, intrinsic motivation to work with and be surrounded by horses.

Take Laura Kraut for example, when I asked her how she deals with setbacks and difficult moments, she replied; "Again, I go back to, I just love horses! So when you have set backs, like you lose your top horses or something goes wrong. For me as long as I still have horses, it's my life, it's what I do."

Daniel Deusser's motivation to work hard and persevere is simple; "I just like it. I like to think about how to work with a horse and I feel they understand me, that's the part at the end that I like the most."

The love for being around and working with horses boils down to a deep trust between rider and horse. Janika Sprunger described how when faced with the biggest challenges in her career, it was the partnership and trust she build with her teammates that inspired her to do better herself. "For me, when it comes to the big challenges in the sport, like with my best horses Palloubet and Bonne Chance, it helped that I know I could really trust my horse. That gave me a lot of power. You really grow as a team and that gave me so much satisfaction and motivation."

Similarly, Laura Klaphake talks about the partnership and teamwork that is so unique to and what she loves most about this sport. "Whenever I have a bad day for example and I get on the horse, I forget about the rest, it's just me and the horse. Ok it's not a team sport like soccer or whatever but you are a team with the horse and this is really important. I really enjoy cuddling with the horses, having fun and especially being a team. It's not like tennis when you have your racket and afterwards its lying somewhere in the corner, its more like a relationship with a friend."

Jonna Ekberg confessed she loves to win, just like everyone else, but her love for the sport comes forth from a passion for working with horses. When I asked her what she loves about the sport, she answered, "For me, I think the horses. Ok I still love to win but I'm not a rider that wins a lot. Winning for me is more like producing horses and seeing them do well. I love the feeling when you bring a horse up to the highest level and someone can come up to you and say 'oh I never thought that horse could jump a course like that' you know. You did it together with the horse, just the feeling that they do it for you. One of my proudest moments is my best horse had been in France his whole life and nobody liked the horse. The owners gave up a bit, he wasn't going so well, so they wanted to sell him and he came to Stephex. He looked really bad, he was a cute horse but he didn't look well you know. He wasn't moving well and then in the end he was so beautiful, he was muscled, he was trotting good, he was jumping like a superstar you know, like you wouldn't recognize the horse. He was bucking, I was almost falling off everyday 'cause he was enjoying life. For me these things are more important than winning, it makes me more happy. That's really my passion about the sport 'cause then in the end its about working with the horses not just that you have a super good horse that you get to ride and go in the ring and win every time. I have some 8 and 9 year olds now that I have had since they were 6 and when you take them from 6yo classes to 7yo classes, to jumping their first ranking class Grand Prix, those things give me real satisfaction."

Jonna is incredibly hard-working, fueled every day by her passion for horses and improvement. "When you see the horses improve, then you know you are doing something right, that's really motivational."

It has become evident to me that the ones most motivated to train deliberately and consistently, are those most in touch with why they started riding in the first place – the love for horses. Perhaps one of the most powerful forms of purpose for an equestrian, therefore, is staying in touch with your why. Something that is easily forgotten about, but also something easily reconnected with. Another very powerful motivator is the passion for improvement.

Passionate About Improvement

When speaking to the riders and taking a peek into their fascinating minds, one thing became evident, they are all constantly and relentlessly thinking about how to become and do better. Thinking about how to get where they want to be. Most often that means, pondering on how to improve their horses one step at a time and where to find their next superstar.

As we have already discovered in Chapter 1 the riders I interviewed are often in a growth mindset. Constantly focused on improvement and reaching their goals. They get a lot of motivation from competing, after all, they are competitive and goal-oriented. That said, though they enjoy reaching goals, they equally, if not more, value and love the process of improvement.

Interestingly, for these top riders, it didn't really matter what level their horses were at. They just love feeling their horses improve. I and perhaps many of you, expected that these riders only want to compete at the top and therefore only ride horses that are ready for that top level. However, Laura Kraut, Lorenzo De Luca, Jeroen Dubbeldam and Jonna Ekberg all shared with me their love for being the rider that is able to bring out that horse's full potential. No matter the age or the natural abilities or "talent" of a horse, reaching a horses' full potential requires patience, teamwork and for a rider to learn from his horse as much as the other way around. Feeling all that hard work, grit, patience and perseverance come to fruition is what these riders wake up for every morning.

Laura Kraut mentioned; "For me to work a 6 years old that might not even be that promising but just to get on it and try and make it a little bit better that day, is an accomplishment." I couldn't help but push Laura a little in order to better understand how this love for horses impacts her everyday decisions at home as well as at a competition. So I asked her if improvement and the love for horses were more important to her than winning classes. Her answer was unexpected yet powerful. "Well I would like to think not, cause I really do like to win. But if I would have to choose, it would possibly surpass the winning. I really love to win, but I also think that there are times where I feel that winning might not be the best for the situation I'm in with that horse. Where others might want to win at all cost, I have never been that way, which some might say is a bad thing, but I don't feel it that way. I do try to win, but I wouldn't jeopardies the horse for a personal satisfaction of winning. I've never said that out loud. But like the other night, I really wanted to win but when I didn't accomplish that, I wanted to make sure my horse was ok. That's maybe why I have been better at nations cups because I then really want to win because the others are relying on me. I am probably more of a ruthless fighter when on a team than when riding individual."

The equestrian sport is unique in that riders work with living animals every single day. They form a team together with these animals and depend on each other for success as well as for staying safe, as the equestrian sport is considered a high-risk sport. Generally, the bigger the jumps, classes and competitions, the bigger the risk for both horse and rider to get injured, especially in the disciplines of show jumping, eventing and racing. Therefore, knowing how much risk to take and balancing this with the horse's training and development is one of the most important jobs of an equestrian athlete. In Laura's case, her motivation to win is big, but her motivation to keep her horses safe and to manage their risks is equally great.

I asked Lorenzo De Luca the same question I asked Laura Kraut; "*What is your motivation to work so hard and get on the horse every day?*" His answer was very similar in many ways. He too enjoys the process of building a young horse up and stresses the importance of learning from the horse as much as teaching them. Apart from that, Lorenzo too mentions the importance of managing the development of the horse. As horses obviously can't talk, it's not always straightforward to know when to push them to do better and when to be patient and give them time. However, it seems this crucial element of the training process is actually what these riders love the most. Hitting that sweet spot is not easy, but incredibly satisfying when done right. In Lorenzo's own words: "Of course, to ride at the big shows and to be at the top level in the sport is fun and motivating. But I think also, when you have a new project, even a young horse, it can motivate you to work with them. I am so lucky because there are so many good horses here [at Stephex stables], that we always have new projects all the time. Every good rider works their whole life to get to the top. But even when missing a GP horse, when you need to build up a young horse, that can be motivating too. *I think we always need to be hungry to learn from our horses.* Because every horse is different and every horse has a different level or talent. I think in the moment you find the right balance with every horse, like last year I had new horses coming up to step up to a next level and getting good results, but I never went over their limits, I never asked more than they could handle. That to me is motivating. Cause I know that I didn't ask too much from them and got them there at the right moment."

I asked Lorenzo what it is exactly he loves about riding a young horse or a "new project" as he calls it. "Well, if we have nothing behind our current Grand Prix horses, we get into trouble. But also, I like horses, and I like to build them up. I like to see how they learn, how intelligent they are, that is really fun. Like last week at the show in Sentower Park in Opglabbeek (Belgium), I went there with younger horses and I jumped with my 8 years old mare, it was her first Grand Prix and she jumped fantastic and that makes me happy."

What about someone who has won every single championship there is to win? What do they get up for in the morning? In a fixed mindset, they probably wouldn't (or not very early anyway). But Jeroen Dubbeldam is not motivated by merely going to the big competitions and championships. Jeroen is driven by a passion for the horse, a mission to get the very best out of each horse he rides. He told me, "Ah its for me a challenge every new horse for me is a challenge. For me every new horse I start to work on is a challenge to get as far as possible. I have also horses that I know and I feel have a limit somewhere. It doesn't matter. If I can get there and I can be successful at that level, for me it's already a win. That is my passion. That's why you don't see me on all the big shows all year because I'm working with new horses, young horses and in between I also sell [horses]. That process is something that I love. I don't need to be on the show every week, win money. Yeah, I also like to win money but this is what I like to do. I don't need to go from Shanghai to Mexico, you know. I do half of those shows in a year and I'm happy."

When asked what he enjoys most about the sport and thus what motivates Maikel van der Vleuten, he talked about his passion and love for the sport itself and the trill of those moments when all the hard work pays of and everything comes together. "I just like the sport. First of all, from my point of view I just like to work with the horses. If I have talented horse, which at the moment I do, I'm really curious how far I can get with the horse. I really put a goal for myself with a kind of horse and follow that. I really enjoy seeing a high quality horse jumping. I just love to see that. You see a super rider with a super horse winning a GP in a way that's just 100%. Also for myself because, of course I have many good results during the year, but it's also the way you get the result. There are not that many jump offs that you ride and think 'this one is for in the books'. You only have a few of those in a year, and those moments, they are really nice."

Finally, when talking about motivation with Olivier Philippaerts, I challenged him and asked him if he had to choose between results in the ring and improvement on the horse, what would he go for? "I've had that question before. For me, I don't think it's the result at the end of the day that is the most important. When I think about improving things, I don't always look at results. Sometimes I need to improve things. For example, in a class or a jump-off I need to do this, this and that better. I need to get that better, even if I don't win the class, I can still be happy with the progress I made. Sometimes I try to improve myself more, that way I don't look at others, I just focus on constantly improving myself."

In line with the other riders, Olivier's motivation comes forth from a passion for working together with the horse. "I think it's being a combination with your horse. The partnership between horse and rider, nobody exactly knows what the best thing to do is. You can make plans and work on improving yourself and your horses, but in the end, nobody knows exactly what the best thing to do is. For example, if you're doing athletics, if you're an amazing runner, you will always be an amazing runner. But with horses you can be an amazing rider, but without good horses you are nowhere. So it's really important to get a good horse fit and to become a great combination with your horse. To buy a good horse, produce a good horse and win with that horse, it takes years to create that. Especially in our situation, we don't buy horses that are ready to go. We buy them when they are young and then we produce them and bring them to the top level. That gives me the most joy. If I can find a horse, or my father finds a young horse and you have a feeling it's going to be a very good horse, you produce them and then one day you can win a Grand Prix or bring it to five star shows, I think that's when you can say, you did the right thing."

Ironically, even though (or because) these riders are very focused on the process and get great satisfaction from feeling their horses improve and grow into their full potential, these riders get great results and are incredibly successful.

You may wonder, "what if I just love to win and that motivates me?" of course, there is nothing wrong with loving that exciting feeling when all your hard work comes together and you manage to win that class or championship. It's exhilarating and can be a huge driver and motivator. However, this extrinsic motivator (a motivator driven by external rewards), is often not sustainable or enough to help you stay motivated in the long run. Therefore, use this type of drive to set ambitious goals for yourself and then remember to create a clear process of how to achieve those goals. Let's look at creating this type of clarity.

Create Clarity

Once you have taken the time to look back and (re) align with you why, it's time to look ahead and create clarity about where exactly you want to get to. Before you commit to your goals, you first want to know exactly what you are prepared to commit to. For example, many athletes dream of participating in the Olympics one day, but once it becomes clear what all the required actions and sacrifices are to get there, many of us decline. Not many people are prepared to do whatever it takes and that is perfectly ok. There is no right or wrong in that sense. Another example would be, many people, me included, would love to have a six-pack. Not many people, also me included, are prepared to do what's required every day to get that type of body. Therefore, the first step is to list all your desired goals and the actions required to get there and ask yourself if you are willing to go all in.

Setting Goals

Setting goals can feel overwhelming, or add pressure, but when done right, it can actually create peace of mind and laser-sharp focus. So let's do this together.

Step 1

As mentioned above I suggest you take pen and paper and start by writing down all the different goals you'd like to achieve. These can be goals for the long and short term and be for all areas in your life. You could list them as follows:

1   Sport.
2   Friends, (spouse) and family.
3   Health and fitness.
4   Business and finances.
5   Other.

Sports goals:
1   I want to start each round with the right show rhythm.
2   I want to win a 120 and 130-meter class this season.
3   I want to be on the team in at least one Nations cup.

Allow a few days to contemplate and write down all these goals for yourself.

Step 2

Now, list all the actions you can think of per goal. Some goals might be clearer than others in terms of what action they require. Just start with what you know. You can and will add and adjust over time. For example:

Sports actions for goal 1:
1   I need to practice for at least 10 minutes per horse in show rhythm this week.
2   I need to visualize myself riding in this show pace for 5 minutes every day.
3   I need to remind myself to start in the right rhythm before getting on each horse at the show.
4   I need to get into my show pace for at least two rounds in the warm up.

For those goals you have little control over, such as goal number three, wanting to be selected on the team, you may struggle to think of clear actions to take, as being selected is not up to you. I encourage you to think about it anyway. Be creative, what might the chef d'équipe be looking for? Can you find out by talking to someone? Can you do research to get the answers you need? If you would compete very consistently all season, will this increase your chances? If so, how can you make that happen? Write these actions down.

Step 3

Once you are aware of all the actions you need to take to reach your goals, you will most likely end up with a very long list of things to do. Therefore, it's now time to prioritize and decide what you are prepared to do, and what you are not willing to do. Set your ego aside here. Whatever you decide is totally fine. Remember, you can do anything you set your mind to, but you can't do everything all at once with 100% focus. Therefore, it's time to categorize your goals into:

1   Do.
2   Delay.
3   Delete.

The goals in the "Do" list are the goals you can now fully commit to.

Step 4

Finally, take the actions on your "Do" list and plan them into your diary. Make sure you remember to take the required actions, so set reminders if need be.

How the Best Set Goals

Let's take a look at how McLain Ward and Cian O'Connor set and work toward goals. I asked McLain how he prepares for a championship. "Normally on the flight home from the championships I will think about the next one. First, it's got to be a reality that this horse is going to go to another championship. Championships don't come all the time, you know, you have to factor in [your horse's age and health] and then if I decide this is the horse I am aiming toward that championship then I will work absolutely 100% backwards. First what is the scenario to prepare the horse the best for the championships? Then, because that is not the only event of the year, how can I plug in these other events? So you need a grand plan that still allows you to do the sport at a high level. I have left some flexibility since I have gotten older because things change a little bit. For the same reason as the course walk leave a little flexibility so that you are not deviated by the adjustments that need to be made. With horses you have to be a little bit malleable."

In summary, McLain sets his target or big goal and then works backward from there. Planning the shows around what the horse needs to be ready for the championship as well as having a clear and deliberate plan for the training at home. Eventually, they know exactly what they are working on over the next month and weeks and these sub-goals become very process-focused. The end goal might be a result goal, but the sub-goals are most often process-focused. Over time, McLain and his team have learned to stay flexible along the way. The end goal is clear, how to get there depends on the horse, circumstances and shows.

Not surprisingly, Cian O'Connor goes about it in a very similar way. "I think with a goal, don't be afraid to aim high. However, you have to be realistic as well. There's no point in somebody with no experience saying 'I am going to go to the Olympics next year.' He/she should say 'I am going to go there in 8 years.' I think you pick your target and don't be afraid to aim high, then work back from it. There are certain stepping-stones. I mean, if I was eighteen again and I was jumping national Grand Prix in my country, the first step is you want to get international exposure. You want to get to international shows. Then you want to try to jump on a larger level: Nations Cup for your country. Then, you keep your horse and your sponsor or owner to try work up over a 5-year period to the top team. Then, from all that experience gathered you try to jump a [5*] Nations Cup. What we see nowadays is people want to compete but they don't really want to train. That is negative for the sport. Really, people have to allow time to say I want to put the best time into my career and I am going to become good at what I do. And then I will compete. You see so many people now [who] want to compete and it's hit and miss. They win one day or they have five down the next day. I think it's so important as trainers [that] we have to be strong enough to say 'you don't need to jump that class and you need to jump a bit smaller'. It's important to educate the rider, to lead their parents that it's about training and stepping to a higher level. You can have short-term success if you buy a fancy horse and the person clicks with it. But to ride multiple horses over 10-20 years you have to work hard for it first.

Yeah, each time along the way without taking the eye off the ball you know if we want to jump the World Championships and a particular show is 6 weeks beforehand and it was a mini-goal along the way but you arrive there and the ground is diabolical then you don't risk the bigger goal. You scrap that one so as not to be afraid to be strong. When you are young you are impetuous you think 'oh, today is the most important day ever'. You have to always keep the bigger picture in mind. The main thing with horses is soundness, whether they are good or bad they can't go anywhere if they are lame. It's really important to have horses not over jumped. You see that particularly in Wellington, Florida people get excited about week 3 or week 4. They get all excited then guess what, in 6 weeks it's over and no one cares so you have to think about bigger things."

Quick recap when it comes to setting goals. First, think about and write down your big dreams and goals. Then work backward from there. The closer you get to your current situation, the more process-based goals you need in order to keep working deliberately toward improvement. Plan your shows around this long-term plan, instead of aiming to win or ride "perfectly" every weekend. In other words, don't be afraid to, like these top riders, think long-term and work on improvement (even during shows if necessary) instead of wanting to "prove" yourself every weekend.

The Power of Commitment

Professor Steve Peters, a Consultant Psychiatrist, specialized in optimizing the functioning of the mind has helped many British athletes and teams understand themselves better and with that, helped them perform better. Peters has created what he calls "the mind management model," which he describes in his book, *The Chimp Paradox*. In this book, he explains how motivation is not enough to reach success. "Motivation generally happens when there is a great reward to gain or when you are suffering so badly that you want things to change. Motivation is helpful to drive us on but it is not essential to success. It is unrealistic to expect to 'feel motivated' every day, no matter what you are doing. The problem with motivation is that it works on feelings from the Chimp [A concept he explains in depth in his book] and these can shift very quickly. Commitment, on the other hand, comes from the Human and does not depend on feelings. Commitment means following a plan even if you don't feel like it that day. For example, a surgeon can't say halfway through an operation, 'Do you know, I just don't feel motivated to finish this, so I'll stop now!' Motivation doesn't matter; it is commitment that will finish the operation."

Motivation is step number one, but commitment is what gets the job done. Knowing why you do what you do is empowering and a great first step, but being committed to do whatever it takes, is what gets you from A to B. Dreaming of your goal is not enough, wanting it really badly, or even visualizing it every day is not enough either. It's the deliberate action you take every day that gets you to where you want to be. Being committed to your goal is not just about being on time every day or working really hard. It's about doing whatever it takes and doing that over and over again with relentless focus. The definition of commitment is; "*the state or quality of being dedicated to a cause, activity, etc.*"[2] This dedication requires integrity to stick to what you need to do, even when no one is around to keep you accountable.

In his book *Straight-line Leadership*, Dusan Djukich, a leadership coach and developer of Straight-Line Coaching technologies says; "What you have been committed to up to now is revealed by what you have produced or have failed to produce. A commitment is not a natural product of any special kind of mind. It does not naturally flow from any sort of personality. It is always a creation. *A real commitment is a powerful declaration that functions to alter behavior.* If performance is the capacity to generate results, then commitment is a promise to what's required to get those results you are after. It is the fuel that runs the engine."

For anyone struggling with the goal setting exercise above, or for those who feel like they are committed but don't have anything to improve upon or anything to achieve, ask yourself; what have I NOT achieved in the last 12 months? or, what have I not yet achieved or am I not happy with in general? The answer to that question is telling, as you wouldn't come up with it if it wasn't important to you. What if, at the end of your career or life, you had still not achieved this thing, would you be disappointed? If so, you know what to do. Say YES to commit 100% to get this done. It doesn't matter if you don't know where to start, just start.

"And" as Djukich puts it "when your days take you into overwhelm, remember this: it's not time management that has you confused; it's commitment management. Because when we aren't clear about what we are committed to, we tend to get over-involved, and this produces what we call "the mess" of not having enough time. There may be many things you are *involved* with but are not committed to. Keep the difference clear. *Because a lack of clearly-defined commitments opens the door to you saying "yes" way too much and "no" not nearly enough."*

Winning Habit Number 6: Start with Why Then Commit to the How

What we have learned in this chapter is that motivation, like confidence grows from within. When we are aligned with "why" we do what we do and stay committed to this passion, we can conquer any "how." If you haven't done so already, take a moment to go back and think about why you started, I encourage you to get pen and paper and do this exercise now. It doesn't need to be perfect, just close your eyes, take a few deep breaths and feel your feet on the ground. Now go back to the first time you saw or interacted with a horse or the first time you thought about your business idea. What excited you about it, what made it so special to you? Allow yourself a few minutes to step into this moment as if you are there again. Smell the air, feel the sunshine, breathe at that moment and feel the awe and excitement again. When finished, open your eyes, give yourself a good stretch and write down whatever comes to mind (or to paper).

Once clear about your why and what sets your soul on fire, it's time to look forward and create clarity by setting goals and become aware of all the actions required to reach those goals. This is a process, stay patient as you follow the steps described above and dare to say no to whatever doesn't really align with your why or doesn't contribute to your happiness or goals.

Now that you are clear on what's important to you, why and how to get there, you can commit to it 100%. Then, as Cian suggested, stay flexible along the way and don't ever stop till you get there. Even if you don't exactly know what all the required actions are yet or don't have the required information yet, figure out what the next step is and take it!

Winning habit # 6 Motivation

- Your unique **"why" gives direction** to your life.
- We must **inspire** ourselves and others in order **to succeed** in the long run, **not manipulate**. The way to do this is to start with the most important question, "why do I do what I do?"
- The riders I interviewed have in common a **motivation** to consistently train hard which comes **forth from a deep love and passion for their horses and feeling them improve**.
- Once you are (re) aligned with your why, its' time to look ahead and **create clarity about where exactly you want to get to.**
- **Set goals** to create peace of mind and **laser-sharp focus. Start by listing** all the **areas in your life** you'd like to set goals for. Then **write down** a **goal(s) per area**, followed by all the **actions each goal requires** to complete or pursue that goal. Now **prioritize** this to-do list into; **Do, Delay and Delete**. Finally, **plan in** your Do actions **and start** straight away!
- **A real commitment is a powerful declaration that functions to alter behavior.** If performance is the capacity to generate results, then commitment is a promise to what's required to get those results you are after. It is the fuel that runs the engine.

Notes

1 www.simonsinek.com.
2 https://languages.oup.com/google-dictionary-en/.

7   Learn from the Best

So far, each chapter has been a combination of theory in performance psychology, wise words from the riders I interviewed as well as my own expertise and experience. In this chapter, however, I have left the stage for the riders entirely. The final question I asked all of them was this one, "What kind of advice would you give young riders to improve themselves and their mental game?" The answers were beautiful gems of wisdom, each one uncovering another glimpse of their own journey and lessons they had to learn for themselves. It may have taken these riders years to learn, yet in this chapter, you get immediate access to all this knowledge. Let's wait no longer and learn from the best.

> *"What kind of advice would you give young riders to improve themselves and their mental game?"*

Focus

Laura Kraut: I work on telling them [Laura's students] all the time, which is, to practice, even when they are getting a lesson, to feel what is going on underneath them and focusing ahead of what's coming. They might be thinking about the course only and not about the horse underneath them, or they are only thinking about the horse but not about the course at all. So really work on being able to do both. Back in the day, we had to be able to tell our trainer stride by stride what was going on and what happened. I could remember if an ear flicked or a tail switch. So we were thought to be that attentive to what happened in the ring.

> *So it's really about the ability to be in that moment and at the same time interpret everything that's coming at you?*

Yes. Like with one student now, she is doing school, she was feeling a lot of pressure to win, and so when she was coming to ride 6 or 7 horses, she wasn't

DOI: 10.4324/9781003204084-7

present with more than one of them. So now she rides 2 or 3 to really be able to focus on her riding.

So it's important to learn more about your horse and finding out something new you didn't know before. Those are the things you have to focus on. That's why I always get my kids young horses, so they learn to appreciate the small improvements young horses make, rather than putting pressure to go out and win. Because those young horses can't win all the time yet. So there is no pressure on them to win only to learn more about their horses, I don't want them to worry about winning!

Laura Klaphake: Never give up. It doesn't matter if it's not going well, the sport is so interesting, one day it's going good the next, not anymore. With the mental thing, you should focus on you and the horse and you shouldn't focus on the other riders at the show, like I want to be better than this one. You should focus on yourself. At the show, it's too late to train more so just focus on yourself and the horse again.

Winning Habit Number 7: Learn from the Best

Lorenzo De Luca: To stay really open-minded, to learn from everyone, open your eyes to watch great riders at big shows. Even if you are not riding yourself, you can learn by watching how they work their horses, flatwork, manage everything in the stables. I think that's very important. And to not get overstressed about the results! The more you want the results, the less you get the results.

Was that a lesson you had to learn yourself?

Yes, before when I reached the jump-off, I would really want to do well and then the over-motivation destroyed what I built up. *So you learned to let go of results?* Yes let go of the results, focus on the horse and don't go over their possibilities. And then everything will come together because your horses can do it and you can do it.

Edwina Tops-Alexander: I think to live and learn from others is the only way to think. It's crucial to stay positive in all situations but being open-minded can make all the difference.

| Daniel Deusser: | As a kid, well still now sometimes, I loved to go to big shows or national shows and watch other people, well the famous riders at that time and watch them in the warm-up. How they warm up their horse, how they ride their horses. Of course, over the years, through meeting and talking to these people, you learn a lot and find out even more." |

Train the Mental Game

| Jonna Ekberg: | I think you have to be aware of it [mental game]. Read about it or be interested in it. I think it's something that you have to be open for. I think there are no rules about how you have to do it. You need to know yourself, have knowledge about it and then I think it can go a long way. Not just like you have a problem, you get stressed or you get so nervous you forget the course, not just I need to get better or I need to remember the course, maybe see a little bit where it is coming from. Working with a mental coach doesn't mean you have mental issues. I think of it more of something interesting you want to learn more about because it is interesting. I read a few books or you can Google something and find more information. You just have to be open to it and think it's just a way to get better. Just like you train your horses, you take them to different places if they are spooky, you get them more calm. That's also mental training in a way. So you just have to be open to it and not ashamed. |

| Piergiorgio Bucci: | To study and to train, training the mind is the most important thing. |

| McLain Ward: | I would give young riders two pieces of advice. First is, if your only reason for doing this is to go to the Olympic games one day, you should pick something else. Because if you don't enjoy the journey and the battle and the competition and all of that. That in itself is not worthy enough, it's not going to be much fun. That [the Olympic games] is the cherry on top and of course that can be the vision that can be the goal. I hear people say how do I get the opportunity to get to the Olympic games one day, be that level of rider? Ok fine put that over there somewhere and you got to enjoy what you are doing. That right there is the first thing, otherwise you are going to be frustrated everyday. As far as the mental game, is to realize, as you said earlier this is a huge mental game and every opportunity |

you have at whatever stage in your life in career/riding you can learn skills, be around people who do that well, people who embrace that, people who teach that, it's only going to make you better. It's certainly not going to take anything away from you. Certainly, people like myself maybe needed it [mental training] more than other people. I don't think it will draw back. You can only improve, so everything that you can maybe do to improve you have to, because somebody else will, right?

Olivier Philippaerts: When you recognize for yourself that you could need some mental help, you shouldn't be embarrassed to ask for it. Cause some people they play it cool and say I don't need it, but you feel yourself if you need it or don't need it. If you do, it's important to ask for it. Our sport is mentally very challenging. We need to be physically fit but for us the mental concentration and focus is the most important in our sport, it's very, very important.

Work Hard and Create Opportunities

Jonna Ekberg: In the end, I think if you are a really hard worker and you show everyone that you want to make it, then it doesn't really matter what level you start at. Be very aware of your reputation. For example, if people talk about you "oh I know that girl, she rides ok but she works really hard" people will like that and then maybe you get an opportunity that you wouldn't have gotten if you had a bad attitude. For example, if someone told you to do something and you were like "no I don't want to do that." I think if people see that at the show that you are working that you are up early. Like me I didn't have a groom till I started at Stephex, that's when I first had a groom. Like before that, I drove the truck and everything. You work so hard for it so people around you see you really want to do this, then I think opportunities will come a lot easier. Even if you get a job when you muck out 20 stables in the morning and ride 4-year-olds, then the person you work for will see that and say to someone "she is working so hard" and they might say it to another one and another one. Then you might get a good job offer cause they know you will do anything to get there. Young people now they come down to countries like Germany, Holland or Belgium and they expect to get a job with horses to jump Grand Prix. But these [jobs] do not exist, you have to prove yourself all the way. You see, hard work and dedication and motivation will take you very far. You just have to wait for the right kind of opportunity to come along.

Cian O'Connor: It's all linked, you can have a good mental game and you can be focused, it all goes hand in hand. It depends on their situation if you are a young guy and you don't have much chance you have to create your own chance. Get up off your backside and go work for somebody who's good. Go and create your own opportunities. When you get those opportunities you are able to take them with both hands. I think it stems from that a lot of people don't want to work hard anymore you have to get stuck in and that first 10–15 years of your life you have to work like hell and challenge your mental game. I think if you are the one that stands out, I could have more than 20 staff, that person that's doing that bit extra in the morning or staying that bit extra in the evening, shows a bit more interest, is a bit more keen trying to learn, you are going to look after that person. That person will get the chance. I think you have to realize that it is hard to make it but you draw opportunities to you. I am a big believer in making your own luck if you are honest and really, really hard working. You see the difference in some staff like you will have some people who really want to do well and then you have others who it's just a job for them, that's hard to get by if it's just a job for you. That lack of passion is seen, then maybe it's not for you. But if I see a guy that wants to do well and he has to push himself again, look at Kent [Farrington] look at his background and when he started. He would tell you stories of watching the ring and picking up old dodgy horses that no one would ride and getting them going. You can make it, it's not a question if it's possible, it's how much you want it.

Janika Sprunger: I would tell them to believe in themselves but also to work for it. You have to work so hard. Don't be overly ambitious. You have to build step by step. I always went step by step because of my father. Pace is the most important. You have to be patient, you're dealing with an animal. You need to care for the horse. Parents pushing young kids to win is not great, they have to work their way up.

Horsemanship and Teamwork

Daniel Deusser: Mentally you get stronger by yourself, you realize the other ones are not different. Maybe they are better because they train better or they are better because they believe more in themselves, but to understand that every rider is the same physically, you cannot do with your hands or legs other things than the other riders, but you can think different. You can have different ideas. You can focus on different situations, on different points. Some riders focus just that the horse has its head down, other riders just that they are in balance, if the head is up or down, left or right, what the horse needs to jump a course, that's what matters. Just think logically. If you can win a class and the horse has its head up, ya then you win with a horse having its head up, better than having a horse with his head down for 12 jumps and having one jump you cannot jump anymore. It sounds complicated but in the end, I think you just have to think very, very simple. What do you need in the ring and then improve that a little bit. You need the gas and brakes, left and right and then you can see, if I was not fast enough, why? Maybe because the horse runs over the shoulder, then you train that a little bit in your flatwork everyday so that the horse is straighter and doesn't go over the shoulder. These are all the things that you can only find out if you think very simply and don't make it too complicated and don't ever try to imitate somebody. I think you need to have your own style, need to think about your own style. You can always learn a little more from the way other riders think and train but never try to imitate them.

Jeroen Dubbeldam: To not step on the horse like a motorbike. Think with the horse in mind and be a team with the horse, put a lot of attention into horsemanship.

How do you become a team with a horse?

By working with the horse and try and make the horse better, try and make the horse more confident, do everything so you and your horse become one. Somebody told me once that this is an individual sport, but it's not, it's a team sport, you're a team with your horse. And if you're not able to work together then the party is over.

Maikel van der Vleuten: In the end, it's important that as a rider you have the right group of people beside you. You can't do everything alone. Yes you are alone in the ring but you need a good team in all kind of cases. Mental-wise, it's also maybe the same. People who support you in the thing they are strong at that gives you as a rider also the right confidence. I think if you find the right person or people to support you, you will have a click with them. And that person knows when he needs to tell you something that you have to do better or when he needs to leave you alone. My father does that very well. He knows that I am very hard on myself when there are things I do wrong. He can see that in me and knows when I need to be alone for a while. He thinks about it [the mistakes] himself and I will speak with him later about it. You will have a feeling with the person. If it is a mental coach or a trainer, it doesn't matter, the people around you should give you confidence. So that if he tells you something about the course, you naturally agree. If eight out of ten times what he's telling you, you do not have a good feeling about, then that doesn't give you the right confidence.

Winning Habit # 7 Learn from the Best

- All the riders interviewed for this book were asked the question; *"What advice would you give young riders to improve themselves and their mental game?"* Their answers are as follows.
- **Focus: feel** what is going on **underneath you** and **focus ahead** of what's coming. Ultimately, the only thing that matters when riding is to **focus on you and the horse.**
- **Learn from the best:** the **most effective way to learn** a (new) skill is to **observe, watch and learn from the best**. The riders I spoke to have all understood this concept very well and mentioned they learned a lot just **by studying other riders' flatwork or warm-up** while at a horseshow.
- **Train the mental game:** be open to improving yourself on every level, including the mind. Read, research and work with a mental coach to strengthen your mental game. As Olivier said; **mental concentration and focus is the most important in our sport.**
- **Create opportunities:** a **great work ethic** combined with an **eagerness to learn and improve creates opportunities.** In Cian's words, I am a big believer in making your own luck if you are honest and really hard working.
- **Horsemanship and teamwork:** teamwork makes the dream work. This goes for the people around you as well as the partnership between you and your horse. Jeroen said it best, **think with the horse in mind and be a team with the horse, put a lot of attention into horsemanship.**

8   Success

In working on this book, conducting these interviews, and researching the art of peak performance, I have learned how much control we have over our own life trajectory. This is why I called this book *Winning Habits*, as every habit we explored in each chapter is a concept you can learn and make your own. When practiced consistently, these habits can continue to grow stronger from the inside out. On this journey, I have come to realize that even success is something that comes from within. Success is about becoming the best version of yourself and like the legendary football player Pelé so famously said, "Success is no accident, it's hard work, perseverance, learning, studying, sacrifice and most of all, love of what you are doing or learning to do."

In Chapter 5, we redefined failure. Now it's time to look at our definition of success. I suggest, therefore, that we end this book with the beginning in mind. Before setting out to implement all these winning habits, let's explore the concept of success in more detail and ask ourselves this very important question first; "What is success for me?"

Success Defined

When thinking about success, we all have different ideas of what that means exactly. Thoughts such as "being the best," "winning," "running a financially successful business," "having a beautiful house and car" or "having great re-lationships" come to mind. For many, being a successful person means one needs to "achieve" certain things. Yes, the riders I interviewed are often perceived as successful for these same reasons however, this way of looking at success might not be enough nor may it offer a complete picture.

In his book *The Chimp Paradox,* Prof Steve Peters explains the consequences of thinking about success in this narrow way. "If you always wish to measure success in life by what level you attain, then you must accept the emotional consequences when you do not reach this level. If you measure success in life by effort and doing your best, then it is always in your hands to succeed and to

DOI: 10.4324/9781003204084-8

be proud of yourself. So first define success before you start on any venture and also work out what that success will mean to you."

Imagine the following; you have achieved lots and won a championship but are feeling deeply unhappy and lost. What if you have loads of money, a beautiful house and a few cars but still feel unfulfilled or under-challenged at work? Most of us know, money and fame do not make us happy and yet when asked what we want most in life, we answer- "success." Why is that? I believe it's because being "successful" brings about a certain emotion, a feeling of satisfaction. We believe that when we are successful, we are "good enough," accomplished, appreciated and happy. This feeling of "good enough" is what we are after. Feeling good enough will finally help us feel at peace, we have finally arrived. Now we can be happy.

The reality is quite different. Take the most decorated Olympian in history for example. He has won a staggering 28 Olympic medals, but during a mental health conference in Chicago in 2018, Michael Phelps shared how he had struggled with depression for many years, especially after coming home from the Olympic games. He explains in a CNN interview; "The "hardest fall" was after the 2012 Olympics, said Phelps. "I didn't want to be in the sport any-more. I didn't want to be alive anymore." What that "all-time low" looked like was Phelps sitting alone for "three to five days" in his bedroom, not eating, barely sleeping and "just not wanting to be alive," he said.[1]

In his bestseller Open, Andre Agassi describes his love–hate relationship with tennis, which started as a young boy forced to hit hundreds of balls a day. His main goal in life (or perhaps his father's) goal was to win the US Open tournament. Agassi wins the US Open in 1994 and in April 1995 he ranks as the world number 1. In his book, Agassi describes how, after hearing the news of becoming the number one ranked tennis player in the world, he felt nothing. He wonders, "If being number one feels empty, unsatisfying, what's the point, why not just retire?"

These are just two examples of iconic athletes who struggled mentally, even after achieving incredible wins. It begs the question, do these achievements make us feel fulfilled? Or, is it possible to start with the end in mind and create this feeling of fulfillment and enjoyment already right now, wherever you are today and from there continue to achieve great things? Just like confidence, feeling happy, good enough and successful starts from the inside out. Not the other way around.

If you can't feel grateful, successful or good enough right now, the chances of you suddenly feeling all this after a win, will be small or at least, short-lived. Though if we practice feeling confident, good enough and even successful on a regular basis, we will shape it before we make it. Like Tony Robbins says, it's not enough to just chase goals if you can't feel grateful for what you have (achieved) already. It is also not enough to just feel grateful and not have anything to work toward. We as human beings thrive on growth and progress, so if we combine these two forces, imagine the incredibly fulfilling lives we could lead. If we can feel successful today, all the accomplishments in terms of wins, reaching goals or hitting targets will be a bonus. This reduces the pressure to pursue success and instead allows for a lot more fun *being* a success.

Being Successful Today and Even Better Tomorrow

Some of you might be thinking, but I haven't achieved anything yet, I'm still so far away from my goals, how can I possibly feel successful already? The answer is simple; stop chasing and start feeling like it now. If you only look into the future and constantly remind yourself of all the things you still need to do and accomplish, then every day feels like a race. Instead, what if you have already arrived? Take a moment to look back, where were you 10 years ago? What were your skills like back then? What were you like as a person? What kind of rider or athlete were you? Have you since achieved some of the goals you had at the time? If you could tell your 10-year younger self about all the things you would accomplish and the person you would become, do you think she would feel proud and successful? Even for those of you who have had a tough past 10 years, you are probably a much stronger person for it.

Consistent Success

What I've come to realize through writing this book is that success is a matter of perception. If you don't feel successful, change your definition of success. When preparing for my first interview with Laura, I didn't have any questions prepared around the topic of success. However, toward the end of the conversation, it just popped in my head and I had to ask the same question I asked you at the beginning of this chapter, "what is success for you?"

Laura's willingness to be vulnerable and answer the question in a very honest way encouraged me to continue asking the same question to the other riders I would interview. As you will see, the way they answer this question says a lot about them and their perception of success. In my view, there is no right or wrong way to define success, there is only helpful and not helpful. If your definition or perception works for you, great, keep using it. If it doesn't, then make sure to change it.

For Laura Kraut, success means being consistent. This was not an answer I was expecting from one of the leading female riders in the world. She said; "For me right now success is maintaining where I am in the sport, I hope I am able to finish off my riding career staying at a level that makes me feel good. Obviously that relies on the horses you have. I guess accomplishment for me is having and finding the horses that are good enough to keep me there. That to me is an accomplishment."

Is that more powerful to you than winning?

"Yes, it is more powerful to me and right now means more to me than some of the victories I have had. Right now I have some of the best horses I have ever had in my whole career and 2 of them I bought when they were 5 and now they are 10 and they are amazing Grand Prix horses. I have an amazing feeling of accomplishment for that."

Laura's consistent and deliberate training over the years continues to pay off with a consistent supply of horsepower for her to stay at the top of the sport. Success then is not just about winning a Grand Prix on the weekend, it's what you do in between, from Monday till Friday that creates consistent success.

Similar to Laura, Janika Sprunger finds her fulfillment in the day-to-day work created together with her horses, while pursuing achievements and ribbons, it's the everyday work that brings a feeling of success. Janika understands perfectly the concept we explored above, the power of being grateful about where you are today and the exciting feeling of stretching yourself to be even better tomorrow. "For me this [being at shows] is a big success as well. For me, success is not just to win. When I know me and my horse tried our best and we are placed or did just really well that day, this is being successful to me. I try to be happy regardless, not only when I win classes. Ok it [winning] can push you to do be the best as an athlete, but you also sacrifice a lot as well."

It sounds like your bond with your horses is very important to you, is that correct? "Yes indeed, ok if on top of that you can have some success, of course that is amazing. But I also really enjoy the work with my horses, and I work with them every day. Sometimes it can become a bit like working in a factory, that doesn't work for me. For me, my job starts not only when I ride into the ring but it starts on Monday. I enjoy what I'm doing a lot! As long as you still have wishes and dreams, that's really good."

Jonna Ekberg's definition of success is clear and simple; "I think improving myself and the horses, that's success. For me, I think success is working for something and getting somewhere like it doesn't really matter what it is but you taking the next step forward. Slowly, but all the time moving in the right direction. That you are improving yourself and your horses I think that is success."

Daniel Deusser touches on something we will explore later on in this chapter, the difference between getting to the top and staying there. "What is most challenging at the end is not to get to the top but how long you can stay in the top 10 of the world. Being there for 6 months, a lot of people can do that. They buy their way up and they go to the shows. But one that can stay for years and years in the top 10, top 15, top 20 in the world, that's a different story. There are so many good riders but if you can stay consistent at the international competitions and you have results with different horses, then you must be doing something right otherwise it wouldn't work." Again, success to these riders is simple (yet far from easy), it's staying consistent.

You are one of those riders that is consistent at the top, what is the most challenging for you to stay there? "What is most important is to try to apply your system with different horses, build them up so that you stay there. It's just, how do you try to understand the horse, how do you try to train the horses. If the horse is willing to train with you and you are good enough and your ideas are there, I think you will always come back."

I asked McLain Ward and Cian O' Connor a slightly different question, namely, *What do you think is most important to succeed in this sport?* Their answer? Have a clear system, focus on the process and work deliberately toward your goals. Then, and only then will consistent results follow.

McLain said, "It's not one thing, you have to understand to put a bunch of things together. One thing is no longer in any sport good enough. You have to have a sprinkle of talent, sprinkle of opportunity, discipline, and work ethic. Look, for the Olympic dream you need a little bit of good chance, good luck. I should have never had Sapphire or Azur. I turned both of these horses down, and then they came back to me. Certain things are meant to be but at the same time through those other skills, you create opportunities. If they didn't come around maybe something else would have come around. It's putting all of these pieces together and having a goal and a vision and a way to get there, that's your best chance. If you don't have that, it's not going to happen. Maybe one horse in one moment but it won't sustain."

Cian O' Connor, in line with the others, talks about the importance of consistency and the stepping stones toward this consistent success. "I think to succeed in the long-term it's important to have very good basics. For instance, with a horse, we would say ok let's start at the bottom. Let's make sure his feet are good, his diaphragm is good, that he's healthy, that he's fit. Then we would do the dressage and we would control him. Then we train in-between poles so we have a system, which we would like to bring the horse into. We can move left or right in that system, it's not rigid we can be flexible. In other words, we have the basics. But if you are a hit and miss rider, you kind of just get on the horse and just ride to win a class here or there. But if you want success over 10 or 20 years at top Grand Prix and Nations Cup, or Olympic level, **the most important thing to be successful at the highest level, is to have a good basis and have a structure in the work that you do.** You will see people be able to win classes on and off, but they never tend to spend 30 years in the top level or succeed at championship or Olympic level because they don't know how to deliver on the big day. You can look at anybody in all different sports, you hear a guy say, 'on that day in 6 months I am going to be ready'. Obviously, it's harder with horses cause they could get a knock in the lorry, or they are lame or a stone bruise or whatever but I honestly believe if you can build up to the big day, it's a big help."

Finally, Jeroen Dubbeldam shows us that our definition of success and our "why" can be the same thing. Feeling successful in the equestrian sport is all about the horses you ride. Jeroen's, in a way selfless definition of success or purpose in life, is to bring out the true potential of each horse. "For me success is, what I just said before, not all horses can jump Olympics, but if I have a horse whose limit is 1.45 m or two-star GP and I get to that limit and I feel this is what is in the horse and not more and I can be successful at that level with the horse, that for me is success. Because then I have, with that horse, reached the highest possible. Then for me, I've made a success. Of course, the nicest is if that is at an Olympics but I can also enjoy a two star show with a horse that is not capable of doing more and be successful at that level. I go to that show, I enjoy and have a good feeling, I can enjoy."

In summary, to the top in equestrian show jumping sport, success is consistently working on and enjoying the process of improvement which allows the true potential of the horse-rider combination to come out. Jeroen Dubbeldam reminded me that this sport is a team sport, it's about the interaction between horse and rider in such a way that the smallest gesture is enough to understand each other.

Being Successful Versus Staying Successful

As the riders above already made abundantly clear, many people can have successful moments, but to them, success means not just getting to the top but staying there. It's simple; consistent training and thinking creates consistent success, or to quote the legendary basketball coach John Wooden, "Ability can get you to the top, but it takes character to keep you there." What happens once we do reach our goals, or our dream becomes a reality? Many athletes have achieved incredible feats only to disappear from that level as quickly as they arrived. So how do we not only become the best version of ourselves but also stay that way?

I've witnessed over the past 10 years as a mental coach how most of us tend to stop doing what works. When clients come to me, they are very hungry for change. They will do anything to reach their goals. Most of them use the tools and lessons learned consistently and start to see great results. However, I also noticed that for many clients, once they reached their goals, they stopped doing what works. Let's be honest, many of us, including myself in the past, stop doing what we need to do, even if we know that what we're doing works. We stop doing our daily meditation or yoga or reflection at the end of the day, we stop training deliberately and go back to autopilot. Success breeds complacency. Therefore, in order to stay successful, it's crucial to keep doing the work, to keep reinventing yourself to constantly get and do better. That work should never stop, the moment you do, you don't plateau as many believe, you go backward. That is why you see the best in any industry, from athletes to Michelin chefs, to entrepreneurs find ways to stretch themselves even further, to dig even deeper, also once they have already achieved outstanding success. Those deeply immersed in the growth mindset can't think any other way, they are so obsessed with improvement, learning and becoming an even better version of themselves, they are willing to let go of everything they have achieved thus far, they are willing to let go of that version of themselves in order to become someone even better.

When you stay focused on the process, using deliberate training and the other habits in this book, you will create your very own roadmap to success. This way, no matter the circumstances or level of failure or success, you can always find your way back to consistent, ever-growing success.

The Roadmap to Success

Let's take a look at how we can use the habits learned in this book to become more consistent and form a roadmap for you to not only reach success, but also to sustain it.

1. Prepare

The first step in this process is always, preparation. We all know the phrase, "if you fail to prepare, you are preparing to fail," so take a moment now to go through the habit summaries at the end of each chapter to remind yourself again of all that you have learned. Using a growth mindset to shape the way you approach your (riding) career and everything else that's important to you means you are not afraid to get it wrong, rather excited to continue to learn more. With this new mindset, you see training in a very different way, if you haven't already, make sure you write down the deliberate training goals for your riding, mental and physical skills for both you and your horse(s). Then plan them into your diary so you won't forget to implement and check off once achieved.

2. Practice

Once your preparation is in place, it all comes down to the action you take. A plan without action is just a wish. Anyone can make a plan or set goals, but consistently taking action is what creates results. Focus is the key here, a half-hour deliberate and focused training session is better than a 1-hour training on autopilot without clear objectives. It's not enough to just go through the motions, again in order to create consistent results, we must train consistently with focus and a deliberate plan. Stay consistent in your training and you will start to see consistent results at the shows, and this doesn't just apply to your horses' skills. Remaining a student in life, staying hungry and foolish as the late Steve Jobs so famously concluded, is what breeds a relentless, consistent and successful life. No matter what level you are at right now, you can always improve your mental game, physical body and riding skills as well as people and horsemanship skills or anything else you need to get to the next level. Staying open-minded as Edwina Tops-Alexander taught us and being willing to learn from others will contribute to becoming a well-rounded rider who is ready for consistent success.

3. Patience

Lastly, we must practice the art of patience. Patience is often overlooked as an important mental skill. Now that you have prepared yourself and are practicing consistently, allow time for the training to translate into effortless skills. Remember Lorenzo's words, "Don't get overstressed about the results! The more you want the results, the less you get the results." **This is the time to trust, let go of the outcome and immerse in the process of being a successful rider and training like one**. At this stage, you might be doing all the right things and still not be getting the results you are after. Stay patient! Laura Klaphake explains in her own words how the sport requires patience, "I think the most important thing is to train at home and if it's not working out, go to a show and ride smaller classes. The most important thing is to be patient then. It takes time, you can't force it. You can't train 5 times a day and say ok it's better." Laura is right, you can't force the process of excellence, rather you want to commit to it without attaching to the outcome. As we learned in Chapters 1 and 5, when in a growth and confident mindset, we turn failure into feedback which leads to real freedom. Think about it, when you fully surrender to the process, stay focused and are not afraid to fail, you have already succeeded.

Feeling Successful Already

To me personally, success is feeling grateful for where I am today and to continuously strive to be even better tomorrow, to enjoy this journey and pass on and share as much as possible, the knowledge acquired along the way.

Now it's your turn, take a moment to get pen and paper. Take three deep breaths and answer the questions below to create your own definition of success.

1   What does success mean to me?
2   What will change or happen once I reach this success?
3   How does this idea of success make me feel?
4   Why is this success so important to me?

5   What would life look like if I was already successful today?
6   What would that feel like?

Take this feeling and image of *being successful* and step into it as if it's already happening right now.

Stepping into a successful life comes with responsibilities. Everybody wants to reach success, but not everybody is willing to do whatever it takes. We often already know what we should do to improve but knowing is not enough. You can read all the self-development books out there and never evolve. The power of knowledge lies in applying it and then living it. One thing I know for sure is that if we live these seven habits outlined in this book and if we adopt a growth mindset and a focused and deliberate approach toward creating excellence, we will step into our true potential and live a life in flow.

So go live those habits and see for yourself how your life will transform.

Winning Habits

- Before setting out to implement all the winning habits learned in this book, ask yourself this question first; **"What is success for me?"**
- Just like confidence, **feeling successful starts from the inside out**. If you want to experience success, you have to start by **feeling successful already.** This reduces the pressure to pursue success and instead allows for a lot more fun *being* a success. From there you don't stop training to **become even better.**
- To the top in equestrian show jumping sport, **success is consistently working on and enjoying the process of improvement** which allows the true potential of the horse-rider combination to come out.
- **Preparation, practice and patience** form the **roadmap** for sustainable and consistent success.

Note

1 https://edition.cnn.com/2018/01/19/health/michael-phelps-depression/index.html.

Conclusion

This book has come forth out of a desire to answer questions. To discover what habits and patterns the best of the best in equestrian show jumping sport have in common and what their journeys have been like. I started this project therefore with three key questions in mind:

What are the determining factors or characteristics that make the difference for these riders? What do these riders have in common? And, if other riders apply the same habits, patterns and ways of thinking, can they move forward and become successful as well?

I have summarized the key points of this book below, which answer the first two questions; what do these riders have in common and prove to be the determining factors that helped them become successful.

First of all, the riders I interviewed have adopted a winning mindset, meaning they have subscribed to beliefs that helped them move forward, improve and grow. These beliefs are based on the idea that we have the potential to improve, there is no limit to this potential, apart from the one in our own mind. Therefore, in order to keep improving, one needs to stay aware of the (limiting) thoughts, stories or beliefs arising in the mind, train all skills (not just riding techniques) deliberately, consistently and (just) outside the comfort zone.

Just like the brain, the body too has a limitless potential to adapt, learn, and improve. Using deliberate training allows you to shape this potential in any way you like, to reach any goal you set, and to do things you were not able to do before. Or like the late Anders Ericsson says, "learning is no longer just a way of fulfilling some genetic destiny; it becomes a way of taking control of your destiny and shaping your potential in ways you choose."

However, only if your training includes the following: (1) effective training techniques, (2) training outside the comfort zone, (3) well-defined, specific goals, (4) full attention, concentration and conscious actions, (5) correct feedback, modifications of effort and independent thinking, (6) detailed

DOI: 10.4324/9781003204084-102

mental representations or mind maps and (7) a step-by-step approach to building skills. These fundamentals can be applied to training the mind, the body and the horse, creating a lifestyle of consistent and deliberate learning and improvement. Although putting in many hours of focused training outside your comfort zone is challenging, it is also incredibly rewarding.

The quality of our training and performance in the ring very much depends upon our ability to stay focused in the present moment, feeling what's happening underneath you so you know what to do next.

Doing this requires incredible awareness and the ability to catch yourself when you begin to lose focus. Once distracted, (which happens to all of us including the ones at the top) beating yourself up or thinking about what happened will only contribute to the distraction. Instead, it's key to immediately get back to the focus point. Think one step at a time, one jump at a time. Only in the present moment are we able to feel the horse moving and fully absorb the big and small messages it's trying to convey.

As a result of this focused way of training and being able to stay present when riding, the experience of flow is created. Flow is a state of consciousness where one becomes totally absorbed in what one is doing, to the exclusion of all other thoughts and emotions. Flow is more than just focus however, it's a harmonious experience where mind and body are working together effortlessly, leaving the person feeling that something special has just occurred.

Effective riders have learned to prepare themselves as best they can, regardless of how they are feeling. To control what they have influence over and do this routinely. They prepare mentally with visualization, physically with breathing, stretching or running and they prepare their environment like the horse, tack and team members. Finally, they let go and trust that they are ready. Regardless of flow coming naturally or not, everybody can learn to get into flow by finding the unique sweet spot between relaxation and focus, effort and ease.

The number one reason we don't get into or stay in flow, is our reptilian brain. It is wired to focus on anything that may be potentially dangerous or negative to us. In order to stay confident, we need awareness of which part of our brain is calling the shots- our rational neocortex, or our emotional reptilian brain. Secondly, we need to know how to shift when the reptilian brain is controlling our thinking, actions and results.

This awareness and ability to step out of emotional thinking creates the type of confidence that doesn't depend on circumstances or rise and fall in accordance with results. Other ways to create consistent confidence from the inside out are; taking deliberate and consistent action towards your goals, using helpful (body) language, focus on a helpful perspective and step into your authentic power. Finally, when we see failure not as proof that we are no good, but as feedback to how we can get better, it contributes to embracing our journey towards lasting inner confidence and success.

For the riders I interviewed, the motivation to consistently train hard comes forth from a deep love and passion for their horses and feeling them improve. Anyone looking to stay inspired and motivated on their journey needs to have a clear "why" they do what they do and create clarity about where exactly they want to go.

Last but certainly not least, the top riders I interviewed have all committed fully to their goals. More than that, they have committed to who they need to be in order to reach those goals. "If performance is the capacity to generate results, then commitment is a promise to what's required to get those results you are after. It is the fuel that runs the engine."

These riders have helped shape my thinking in that they created context, confirmation and clarity to the research I had done into peak performance. A few answers in particular really stood out to me when I asked them their final question; *"What advice would you give young riders to improve themselves and their mental game?"*

These answers all revolve around two important keys to success for an equestrian. An important cornerstone to becoming a successful rider is – horsemanship.

"It's important to learn more about your horse and finding out something new you didn't know before. Those are the things you have to focus on."

"Put a lot of attention into horsemanship, by working with the horse and try and make the horse better, try and make the horse more confident, do everything so you and your horse become one. Somebody told me once that this is an individual sport, but it's not, it's a team sport, you're a team with your horse. And if you're not able to work together then the party is over."

"Let go of the results, focus on the horse and don't go over their possibilities. And then everything will come together because your horses can do it and you can do it."

The second key to becoming successful in any field is – a powerful mind.

"To study and to train, training the mind is the most important thing."

"You can make it, it's not a question if it's possible, it's how much do you want to."

"Maybe they are better because they train better or they are better because they believe more in themselves, but understand that every rider is the same physically, you cannot do with your hands or legs other things than the other riders, but you can think different."

It has become clear that in order to become a successful equestrian, you have to constantly train to be better every day, developing your mind to become an effective leader and horseman.

Finally, true freedom and living a successful life begins when we can feel grateful for how far we have come, successful in who we are today and excited about what's yet to come. Just like confidence, feeling successful starts from the inside out. This reduces the pressure to pursue success and instead allows for a lot more fun *being* a success.

We are now left with one final question to answer which is, if riders not yet at the top of the sport apply these same habits, can they too become successful? I have helped hundreds of riders transform their rides and lives. I have seen how these winning habits have helped these riders overcome their fears and break through their old ways of thinking. I have witnessed how their results, confidence, motivation and enjoyment increased the moment they started not only understanding and applying these habits, but really *living* them. I know therefore the answer to this final question is a very clear yes and I'm excited to see what will happen when you too immerse yourself in training your brain, making these habits your own, and *living* it.

Author's Note

My journey toward becoming the mental coach I am today started on a Sunday afternoon in 2002. I was lying in bed, crying, feeling a deep sense of sadness, disappointment and frustration. I felt like giving up, I was done. I had just come back home from another horse show.

My round had gone well enough, I was clear, until the very last fence. As I had jumped around the course, the pressure had been building up, all I could think about was that I was still clear and I only had two more jumps to go. "Almost there, don't screw it up now Annette" I thought. And with that thought, I jumped into the last line over the vertical toward the last oxer. I forgot to count my strides. In fact, I stopped riding altogether and froze completely. My horse Peppermint, an intelligent, tall grey mare with lots of character and temperament was a real leader. Put her in any field with other horses and she would take over the lead. That's what she did in that very last line on that sunny Sunday as well. As I had stopped giving any instructions, she had decided it was time to take over and as we ended up on a questionable distance before that very last oxer, Peppermint made an executive decision. Which was to stop at the very last moment and with that send me flying over, landing on my backside on the other side of the fence.

Mind you, this was not the first time I froze midway through a course. This inconsistent riding had been going on for quite a few years already. It was therefore not so much my body aching that got me to go straight up to bed that evening. It was my heart aching. I was tired of trying to prove myself, making a fool of myself and I was tired of failing all the time. I knew I had to figure out why I stopped riding like that on course.

After crying nonstop since the moment I got out of the course, thinking I had had enough and I would definitely quit riding, one thought kept coming back to me, "if I'm really so useless at this, and clearly not good enough to become a successful rider, then why can I ride so well sometimes at home?" If I can do it in those moments when nobody is watching and there are no expectations, then is this really a matter of not knowing how to ride, or is this a matter of not knowing how to think?

My tears subsided, I felt like I was on to something. In that moment I decided to find an answer to this question and give it another shot. What did I have to lose? I decided to learn more about my mind and how I could "fix" my "thinking problem" on the horse.

As I mentioned in the introduction, as a result of my decision that day, I started working with a mental coach, started reading more about the mind and eventually studied Applied Psychology. This led to me starting as a mental coach myself 10 years later. I had stopped riding and started coaching. I was loving it and felt like I had finally found my purpose in life. Over the years I would occasionally ride with a friend or when giving a workshop abroad find myself on a horse, exploring the Norwegian countryside or enjoying the Mexican sun. People would regularly ask me, "are you still riding yourself?" and I would answer, "no I don't have time, too busy helping others ride." Deep inside however I knew this was only partly true. I still had unfinished business when it came to my own riding, but I was too afraid to admit it.

When reading my own writing before sending the final version to Melanie, my literary agent, I couldn't help but notice I had described my own experiences throughout this book to help illustrate points or bring things to life, and they were all pretty negative. Over time I have learned to stop being embarrassed and instead embrace my journey as a rider so I can help others do the same. Partly as a result of that, I have helped countless of riders overcome their fears, insecurities and helped them not only enjoy riding again but also be brave and step into their power. After realizing I had done this for hundreds of riders, except myself, I knew I had a decision to make.

I too had to step into my power and onto the horse again. Challenge myself to put all that I have learned into practice and come full circle. Which I did, not long ago. Already within a few lessons I was back jumping some jumps again. It's incredible how quickly muscle memory kicks in, from aching and complaining after the first few rides, my muscles quickly got back into their old shape again. All but one! Being back in the tack has made me realize how much my mental muscle, or my brain has changed since that Sunday in 2002. It has created so many new neural networks, developed in so many ways, helped form so many different ways of thinking and created so many more helpful habits. Though my reptilian brain definitely kicked in a few times, I was able to accept that that is what it does, it tries to protect me. As a result, I was able to keep thinking and with that, keep riding. I also realized again how quickly my brain gets addicted to those great rounds, wanting more of them, and then realize how distracting those thoughts about the result are. Having all this awareness doesn't mean you do everything flawlessly straight away, but you are able to quickly focus your attention from the problem to a solution. I also realized how those rounds when things don't really work out and you keep getting it wrong, are the rides we can learn from the most if we are open to it. But above all, what I have re-learned, is how amazing horses really are! How incredibly intuitive and honest and able to see right through us. We can fool ourselves and other people into thinking we aren't scared, nervous or distracted, but you can't fool a horse. As a result, they are our best teachers. They show us in an instant when our thoughts, focus and body language are not aligned. When we are not in charge of our thinking. When we are not the kind but clear leader we need to be as a rider. I have come to realize how leadership and horsemanship are based on the same principles. Being consistent, deliberate, clear and confident leads to deep, unwavering trust. When we are able to do this for ourselves, we are able to do this for our horses.

I don't know where my own journey with horses will take me exactly, but what I do know is that no matter what, I will continue to remember my why, keep connecting to them in the present moment and keep leaning into trust. What I've learned over time is that it's not enough to merely understand the theory. It's about applying the seven habits consistently and with that, living and becoming it. Doing this has helped me become a leader in my field but above all, it has helped me lead my life in any direction I want it to go.

Acknowledgments

Like any sports performance, it takes a village to reach the finish line, let alone a place on the podium. Similarly, it took the dedication of many to get this book together. I'd like to thank every single person who has contributed in a small or big way. Of course, there are always those who play an exceptional role in that process, and I'd like to thank them more in debt here.

First of all, again a huge thank you to all the riders interviewed for this book. As mentioned in the introduction, elite equestrians travel to competitions almost every single week of the year, so I'm very grateful they were willing to make time to talk to me. You have helped shape my thinking and challenge my beliefs about how successful equestrians think and become successful.

Then there are the experts in Performance Psychology which I quoted in this book such as Carol Dweck, Anders Ericsson, Daniel Goleman, Mihaly Csikszentmihalyi and Matthew Syed. I'm forever grateful for their work and the lessons shared in their books. They obviously had a huge impact on my thinking and with that, the seven habits in this book.

A huge thank you to my agent Melanie Michael-Greer for taking on Winning Habits and help get it to the next level, I couldn't have done this without you, Melanie.

Equally indebted I am to Kate Marillat, a great coach and Hay House author herself who has guided and coached me throughout the writing process. Thank you for helping me dream bigger so that more people will be able to benefit from reading this book and for reminding me to apply the habits outlined in this book in moments when I preferred to stay in my comfort zone. To my other badass coach, Veronique Mucha, thank you for showing me how leadership can be applied to daily life and for pushing me outside my comfort zone on a daily basis.

Thank you, Jamie, my husband for your continued support and believing in me and this book, as well as for transcribing some of the interviews. I know you had to put up with a lot when I was being stressed out over all the outstanding bookwork still to be done.

Massive gratitude to Jenn Goddard for going over those first chapters with me, correcting my dubious spelling and rain in those long sentences. Special thanks also to Amy Collinson and Paige Jacobs for your support in transcribing most of the interviews and giving me feedback along the way. Thank you to all my dear friends and proofreaders; Lexi Carter, Mariel Aguirre, Matthieu David and Claudia Verburgt. for the invaluable feedback and for brainstorming with me on the title.

Thank you also Joanna Catani, for always being there if I need any guidance or support. Thank you Noelle Floyd for getting me started and for organizing the first interview with Laura Kraut.

Last but not least, THANK YOU to all my wonderful clients and the horses I have been fortunate to encounter. For they too helped me become the person and coach I am today.

Book Recommendations

Hungry to continue reading after Winning Habits? Here is a list of books I highly recommend you read as well:

1 Mindset – Carol Dweck
2 Straight-Line Leadership – Dusan Djukich
3 Peak – Anders Ericsson
4 Black Box Thinking – Matthew Syed
5 Focus – Daniel Goleman
6 Flow in Sports - Mihaly Csikszentmihalyi and Susan Jackson
7 The Chimp Paradox – Prof Steve Peters
8 Limitless – Jim Kwik
9 The Athletic Brain – Amit Katwala
10 Grit – Angela Duckworth
11 Bounce – Matthew Syed
12 Talent is overrated – Geoff Colvin
13 Relentless – Tim S. Grover
14 Whole Heart, Whole Horse – Mark Rashid
15 The 7 Habits of Highly Effective People – Stephen R. Covey
16 The Power of Habit – Charles Duhigg
17 Presence – Amy Cuddy
18 No Limits – Michael Phelps
19 Open – Andre Agassi
20 Rafa – Rafael Nadal
21 Gold – Nick Skelton
22 Total Recall – Arnold Schwarzenegger
23 The Golfers Mind – Bob Rotella
24 Sleep – Nick Littlehales
25 Just Breathe – Dan Brule
26 The Four Agreements – Miguel Ruiz
27 Start With Why - Simon Sinek
28 Why We Sleep - Dr. Matthew Walker

Index